THE
Career
Engagement
Game

Shaping careers
for an agile workforce

ANNE FULTON & JO MILLS

First published in 2014
by Fuel50
PO Box 91009
Victoria Street West
Auckland 1142
New Zealand
www.fuel50.com

A catalogue card for this book is available from
the National Library of New Zealand.

ISBN: 978-0-473-29992-7

Produced by PressGang, Auckland
www.pressgang.co.nz

Printed in China through Asia Pacific Offset Limited

Contents

Introduction: The Business Case for Career Engagement

 Aligning employees' values, goals and aspirations with those of the organization is the best method for achieving the sustainable employee engagement required for an organization to thrive 🖢
— EMPLOYEE ENGAGEMENT REPORT[1]

The business case for increasing employee engagement has been built over the last few years by numerous local and global engagement studies. Consider the evidence from workplace surveyor JRA showing a 10 percentage point engagement index increase associated with an increase of $12,130 in earnings per employee.[2] Global research supports these findings, linking engagement to productivity, with organizations that have low employee engagement showing a 44% below average shareholder return.[3]

Even more recently, career development best practices have been shown to be directly related to better organizational financial performance and increased revenue per employee, along with a raft of improvements in HR metrics, such as lower voluntary turnover and reduced absenteeism.[4] This research highlights that the investment in your employees' career development will have a direct impact on your business outcomes and improved all-round organizational performance.

The Career Engagement Game is dedicated to showing how building a best-practice career engagement framework in your organization will help you as an HR practitioner or business leader to achieve better outcomes, while also making a positive impact on your employees' working lives and careers. This investment in your people is a high pay-off activity and benefits all your stakeholders.

INVESTING IN CAREER DEVELOPMENT
In this book, we will show you:

- How to achieve better outcomes by empowering your employees to create great careers with your organization

- How to enable your leaders to deliver better quality conversations

- How to enable your HR team to transform the career experience within your organization while also delivering a bottom-line impact

Career engagement continues to be a key pillar in the engagement proposition and a strategy for achieving significant business return. The following points illustrate how critical an internal career engagement strategy is.

- The top engagement driver for employees is a clear career path.[5]

- The top factor influencing job satisfaction is "more opportunities to do what I do best."[6]

- The top two reasons people stay are "My work. I like the work I do" and "My career. I have significant development of advancement opportunities here."[7]

- The top attraction driver for highly engaged salespeople is opportunity for advancement, with "my manager understands what motivates me" as a top three retention driver.[8]

- To retain the highly engaged customer services individual, career development is essential.[9]

- Engaged employees stay because of the value they give and for the value they receive.[10]

- Nearly 30% of highly engaged employees are either leaving or open to other job offers at any time.[11]

Talent management and its core component, career development, need to be an integral part of the strategic-planning process if an organization is to compete on a global landscape. This is especially the case in a world where there is increasing demand for business agility and career agility in employees. The best companies are already preparing their talent strategies for the 2020 workplace. We observe organizations such as IBM, AMEX, Citigroup and Deloitte leading the way in developing career engagement frameworks. Other businesses such as Amazon, W.L. Gore & Associates and Google are challenging the thinking about how we work, in order to be prepared for a 2020 way of working.

Increasingly, we see many thought-leading Fortune 100 and Best Places to Work organizations building career development frameworks that are integral to their strategic growth plans. The critical role that career development is playing is based on the premise that an organization's performance is dependent on its people. Therefore, talent management and development tactics will be vital to the organization's competitive edge and viable future. Talent actualization and its core component, career actualization, are going to become critical organizational competencies. They will be defining factors in those organizations that will continue to compete successfully in our fast-changing world.

> **Talent actualization and career actualization will be defining factors in those organizations that will continue to compete successfully in our fast-changing world.**

WHY WE WROTE THIS BOOK

We have worked with many organizations of all sizes from the micro to the enterprise organization and we have seen a process that creates synergy between the individual purpose, values and talents of every employee. This synergy can be unleashed to deliver business productivity, performance, retention and engagement benefits. We believe that talent actualization is going to be a defining factor in future business performance and that career management capabilities across the organization will be a key contributor to that actualization. We wanted to share some personal stories of how improved organizational performance is achieved through best-practice career management and some case studies, both individual and organizational, of where these benefits have been delivered. Most importantly, we wanted to provide a simple "playbook" for HR practitioners, CEOs or any line manager that can enhance the motivation and performance of their team or the entire organization. Ambitious, yes, but we have many stories to share of accelerated career success for individuals as well as of organizations that have seen a measurable rise in engagement across thousands of employees through using these techniques and guidelines to unlock potential.

fuel
50

Part 1: The Business Case for Career Engagement

We begin **Part 1** by sharing the business case for career engagement and tackle this from four key perspectives. The first chapter, **The Business Case for a Career-Agile Workforce**, explains some of the global trends that are contributing to a rapidly changing world and why agility is important to leading organizations today and why career agility is important to every employee. We continue the case for career engagement in **Chapter 2, The Retention Business Case**, by looking at current trends impacting retention in organizations, and how the talent wars first predicted by McKinsey & Company are now being revisited in an accelerated and more challenging way.[12]

Chapter 3 looks at engagement trends themselves and articulates some of both the pain of disengagement that is endemic in many organizations globally and the benefits of engagement to a business. We also investigate the compelling link between career development and engagement. We discuss how, with career development as the top driver of engagement globally, leading organizations are investing in becoming smarter about their career development frameworks and how they are communicated to all employees in an incredibly personalized way that impacts engagement. We explain how creating engagement in a single employee through scalable career propositions can create a bushfire of engagement across the organization. We also share, in **Chapter 4**, how the role of the leader can impact engagement and retention outcomes through the reframing of the performance review, with the power of the career conversation to drive enhanced performance and the delivery of customized retention propositions.

Part 2: Individual Tactics for Career Engagement

In **Part 2** we present some of the fundamental principles and career frameworks that underpin an organizational career path program for employees. In **Chapter 5, Shaping Career Value Propositions and the Concept of Career Capital**, we explain how these two concepts are a core foundation for any organizational career program. Career value propositions are an extension of employer branding and the employee value proposition. We demonstrate how articulating unique career value propositions for each employee can impact your HR metrics. We also explain how investing in building the career capital of your employees can create a stronger "psychological contract." This may cost your organization little or even nothing, but it builds a joint venture mentality with your employees that delivers stronger organizational commitment and enhanced motivation.

In **Chapter 6, Work Shaping — Micro Tweaks for Macro Impact on Engagement**, we introduce how the academically recognized techniques of job crafting, or work shaping as we describe it, can be applied easily by your leaders and managers. This is done by delivering micro tweaks to individual employee work experiences for macro impact on engagement. Work-shaping principles can also be applied at a more strategic or macro level for employees with career-shaping principles. We discuss this in **Chapter 7, Creating Career Engagement — Hitting the Individual Career Sweet Spot**, showing how to impact individual career engagement by understanding personal values, motivated talents and individual passions and career preferences. Simple tips are shared on how to leverage these motivational aspects, with and without technology enablers. These best practices can be applied immediately by leaders and HR practitioners, or even by individuals wanting to identify their own career sweet spot.

In **Chapter 8, The Pathway Challenge**, we share a new way of looking at career pathways. The flat organizational world in which we now live, and the increased agility that is needed as we head towards a 2020 way of working, will require a fresh approach to supporting career pathway management for your employees.

Part 3: Best-practice Organizational Principles for Career Engagement

In **Part 3** we start to explore how organizations can create a career framework and processes that will deliver sustainable and scalable career solutions for the entire organization. They will deliver the return on investment that CEOs, executive stakeholders and HR practitioners are seeking. In **Chapter 9, The Pillars of Career Engagement in Organizations**, we explain how to hit the career sweet spot in organizations through addressing each of the following fundamental factors: communication; capability; compatibility; and contribution.

In **Chapter 10, Organization Best Practices for Transformational Career Engagement**, we review what best-practice organizations are doing to deliver an exemplary career proposition to their business. We look at how each of three key enablement factors needs to be addressed individually and collectively to deliver the right outcomes. These enablement factors comprise: employee enablement; leader enablement; and organizational enablement. When given strategic priority, these three processes can be woven into an organization's HR strategic priorities, often over a three to five-year period, to enable a systematic, strategic, sustainable, scalable and impactful career engagement initiative to be delivered. Customer success stories and individual anecdotes are shared to enable the HR reader to take these principles and build a strategic "career engagement" road map to deliver engagement, productivity and performance improvements to their business.

We have a vision for a 2020 workplace where there is a powerful synergy of purpose between individuals and the organizations in which they work.

We love helping organizations create a highly engaged workforce that delivers real results and bottom-line impact. We know that when people use more of their potential at work they are more productive, engaged and satisfied. We are passionate about creating positive and uplifting careers. We believe that everyone can have better work experiences.

The 2020 workplace is an environment that facilitates and enables people to use and express their full complement of talents. By allowing employees to bring more of their talents to work and align their purpose and values, organizations will meet employees' career needs while delivering value to shareholders, customers, the community and other stakeholders.

We are passionate about creating better workplaces and are on a personal and business mission to positively impact the careers and work experiences of millions of people across the globe.

— JO MILLS

Jo Mills, President of Product & Client Strategy and a founder of Fuel50, was formerly General Manager of Career Analysts which was providing executive strategic career review services to executives globally and innovative career transition and management services. Jo is a domain expert in career engagement, with expertise built in HR roles in large corporates and consulting firms. She has focused her career on the world of career enablement, working with organizations to design strategic career programs that generate engagement uplift and organizational value across three levels: individual empowerment; manager enablement; and organizational effectiveness. Jo is fueled by a passion for supporting workplaces to deliver a meaningful career experience for each employee, and this is regularly seen in both the work she does with clients and the leadership of her own team.

Anne Fulton, a founder of Fuel50 and before that Career Analysts and Talent Technologies, has had a lifelong passion for making a difference to people's career experiences. As an original architect of the Fuel50 CareerDrive and career engagement model, Anne has always been on a mission to impact positively the careers and work experiences of people in organizations. She became a registered organizational psychologist with the express purpose of building a career program that delivered better career experiences for individuals while also positively affecting the bottom-line results of the organizations in which they work. Anne passionately advocates for a transformational career proposition that organizations can use to truly actualize the talent of their employees, and deliver a compelling career proposition that supports the business brand proposition and delivers retention and engagement. Providing career support throughout the employee life-cycle has significant benefits and is a vital paradigm shift from the days of providing career transition support only on redundancy or exiting due to performance issues. Customising career value propositions for employees is becoming the next big thing in the drive for improved engagement, talent development and retention.

It is time we re-thought our responsibilities as an organization to the career development of individuals who work for us. The world has changed and many organizations provide 'ambulance at the bottom of the cliff' type career support to staff, either on demand or at crisis moments, such as burnout or on redundancy. Now organizations need 'career-agile' employees and should be fostering the building of career competencies within their employees from the minute they join as graduates or newly inducted employees, with strategic career interventions at annual or even 90-day intervals. These employees are likely to be career-agile, self-directed learners, with resilience from

having increasing career marketability, as well as more likely to put their hands up for stretch assignments.

— ANNE FULTON

Fuel50's career path platform has been the culmination of a lifelong fascination and work with career coaching and assessment. It is designed to: deliver insight and action to help individuals and organizations deliver uplifts in engagement; allow organizations to maximize their potential by unleashing the talents of every individual; and enable managers to understand the motivators and engagers of every employee across the enterprise.

Anne considers that her greatest talent is in attracting and unleashing the capabilities of highly talented individuals who have shared the passion for unlocking potential in organizations and maximizing the career success of individuals across the globe. The stories of many of the unique career experiences of these Fuel50 team members are also shared in this book, and many of the insights that are now foundational to our transformational processes come from these talented people. Fuel50 today is a business that is collectively focused on a mission to deliver transformational culture change through career value propositions that motivate and engage each employee.

Maya Crawley is one of the most recent Career Engagement team members and shares our enthusiasm for better workplaces that deliver *personal wellbeing to employees that equally creates a great place to work.* As intern organizational psychologist, Maya has been contributing research to support the Career Engagement Best Practices Model, and most recently she published the Global Best Practices in Career Engagement Research paper which demonstrates the positive impact that career engagement practices can have on organizational performance, with statistical validation of the career engagement model developed in Fuel50.

NOTES

1 *Employee Engagement Report 2011: Blessing White, Inc.* Retrieved from: www.slideshare.net/oscartoscano/blessing-white-2011-ee-report.
2 *Employee Engagement ROAD TO SUCCESS*, April 2011, JRA. Retrieved from: www.johnrobertson.co.nz/resources.aspx?cat=9.
3 Hewitt Associates (July 29, 2010). *Percent of Organizations with Falling Engagement Scores Triples in Two Years.* Press release.
4 Crawley, M. and Fulton, A. *Global Career Management Best Practices Research Report.* In Press (2014).
5 *2010 Aon Consulting Engagement 2.0 Employee Survey — U.S.* Retrieved from: www.aon.com/ready/attachments/engagement_2.pdf.
6 *Employee Engagement Report 2011: Blessing White, Inc.* Retrieved from: ww.slideshare.net/oscartoscano/blessing-white-2011-ee-report.
7 Ibid.
8 *Employee Engagement ROAD TO SUCCESS*, April 2011, JRA. Retrieved from: www.johnrobertson.co.nz/resources.aspx?cat=9.
9 Ibid.
10 Ibid.
11 Ibid.
12 The "War for Talent" was first identified by McKinsey & Company, in 1996. For a more recent review see Beechler, S. and Woodward, I.C. (2009). The global "war for talent". *Journal of International Management*, 15, 273–85.

PART A
The Business Case for Career Engagement

1 The Business Case for a Career-Agile Workforce

Career agility in employees is becoming an in-demand currency.

DRIVERS OF THE 2020 WORKPLACE

Remember back in the 1950s when most people had employment for life? With that notion a very distant memory even for the Baby Boomers, now we've been promised five to seven careers in our lifetime, but is that really what our Millennials (those born between 1977 and 1997 and soon to be 75% of the workforce) can expect from their employers?

In the mid-twentieth century, the majority of people had a single employer for life, or at least a single career for a lifetime. However, the Baby Boomers and the Gen Xers among us have had to be agile, and there are not many today who have been untouched by redundancy or the need to re-skill in order to retain employment.

In these early years of the new millennium, we have already witnessed a number of disruptive forces that will be drivers of the 2020 workplace. According to the University of Phoenix Research Institute and the Institute for the Future, there are a number of disruptive forces that are now drivers of change and which will define the 2020 workplace.[1]

These disruptive forces include increased longevity and the impact it has on the workforce; smart new technologies that will change the way we work; the advent of the virtual workforce; and new blended media that is enabling organizations to work in ever more creative, agile ways. Let's look briefly into each of these disruptors.

 By 2025, the number of US citizens over 60 will have expanded by over 70%.

So as life expectancy increases among our population the work expectations and experiences of the workforce are changing as a consequence. The organizations we work with are looking at ways to retain their mature workers who often hold critical skills and knowledge. The future workplace will need to actively seek ways to make the work experience appropriate to the older worker. Fuel50's global Career Agility Trends Research (2013) showed that Baby Boomers were looking for as much work–life flexibility as the Millennial, although in a different way. The Baby Boomers were looking for increased work flexibility and regular reduced hours, whereas the Millennial was more likely to be seeking shorter, more intense career breaks. Gone for the Millennial are the two years' overseas travel experience that the Baby Boomers craved, which are now replaced with the six-week intensive or immersive travel experience.

While researching their book *The 2020 Workplace*, Jeanne Meister and Karie Willyerd interviewed many Millennials who said they already believed the work–life balance concept was long dead. They expect work and life to completely blend together in today's 24/7 world.[2]

Both Millennial and Gen X place a high importance on working for a company that develops both career and life skills. There is no question that Google and Facebook have pioneered this way of working, by allowing people the freedom to work whenever and however they like. Workers can come and go as they please, with every kind of service available to ensure that they can work to their maximum while at work. There is also the belief that work can be fun. No question, it is fun when you play to your talents, having the freedom and autonomy to make valued contributions to your workplace.

The era of the smart system

We are entering the era of the smart system where increasingly technologies enable the way we live and work, and how we live and work in an ever-increasingly blended way. The latest wave of Apple announcements indicates that our phones will integrate more effectively our ways of working, our health and our home life. These smart technologies are making it increasingly easy to work remotely, and the virtual workplace is increasingly a reality in the US and across the globe. Some 24% of all workers in the US in 2014 work at least some of the time from home, and this has increased dramatically year on year, from only 2.4% of workers in 2002.

The productivity and personal benefits of telecommuting are very real, as can be seen in the diagrams below.

FIG 1.1

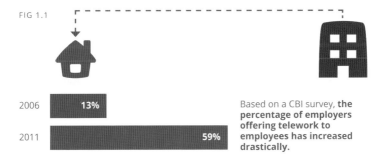

2006	**13%**
2011	**59%**

Based on a CBI survey, **the percentage of employers offering telework to employees has increased drastically.**

In a 2012 white paper, Citrix Systems examined the proportion of employers providing or expanding telework options around the world. They found:

90% USA **85%** China **77%** India **72%** UK **71%** France & Germany

FIG 1.2

The virtual workplace

As a result of the distinctly disruptive impact of smart systems, we are seeing a dramatic rise in the "virtual worker." In 2006, of the 100 Best Places to Work, 79 allowed people to work flexibly, while in 1999 only 18 of the 100 Best allowed employees that option. Virtual workplaces are becoming increasingly commonplace, with these organizations having fewer onsite employees and leaner overheads.

The remote workers are often white-collar workers who have the freedom to work when, where and how they want. Despite these freedoms, we can see that the hours put in and the outputs in terms of both quality and quantity are exceeding those of their office-bound colleagues (see Fig. 1.3). The work outputs can be higher for virtual employees, with 53% of remote workers putting in more than the required 40 hours per week, while only 28% of the comparative "office-bound employees" put in more than their required 40 hours. According to Meister and Willyerd, nearly 40% of IBM's workforce now works virtually. The US is leading the way, with nearly 90% of businesses allowing at least some of their employees the freedom to work from home.[3]

90% of managers believe that works are more productive when given the flexibility to choose when and how they work

Despite the opposition of these major players, the data appears to paint a more positive picture of remote working. According to Inc. Magazine:

79% of workers want to work from home at least part-time

47% female **53%** male — Gender of tele-commuters

53% Teleco-mmuters
28% Non teleco-mmuters
Workers putting in more than 40 hours per week

The work-from-home boom is also having some interesting effects on costs both for employers and workers. Inc. Magazine also reports:

Yearly savings to telecommuting employees

$2,000 $7,000   Mostly on transportation and other expenses

$11,000

Yearly savings to employers

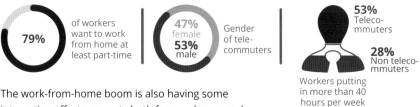

43% of small business leaders report saving of $1,000 or more each month thanks to telecommuting employees

FIG 1.3

There are clear benefits to the employee with virtual working. The average remote employee saves $9,000 per annum largely in travel and parking costs, while the cost savings to employers have been estimated at a conservative $11,000 annually per employee.

It has been suggested that the quality of work outputs can be higher for the virtual employee, with most managers rating the productivity and performance of the virtual worker ahead of that of their colleagues.

Virtual working may be delivering these benefits by offering "flow friendly" work environments that allow people to concentrate on tasks where and when they need to.

New media ecology

We are also entering a world where we have a new way of communicating and a new "vernacular" with blended media combining social media, gaming, virtual realities, video production and media editing that will dramatically change the way we communicate. This will impact on how daily business gets done, and in how we communicate and work together.

Meister and Willyerd describe this as being "hyper-connected." People are connected in more than one medium and simultaneously. Most of us check our phone, LinkedIn, Facebook messages and email practically at the same time and interchangeably. We are entering a future where constant connection is the norm and where our social visibility has increased dramatically. This leaves many of us in a world where we are always "on" to the extent that new "social rules" have had to be created so that there is respect for the person with whom you are having dinner or coffee.

Superstructed organizations

"Superstruct" means creating new forms of organization that go beyond those with which we are familiar. For example, new structures emerge from the application of social technologies. The way work is organized is going to shift over the next decade. We have seen the death of the career ladder and its replacement with the career lattice, and in the new "flat organizations" we will continue to see innovative ways of working together. The likes of Google and Facebook have pioneered the way we work together, with more collaborative, project-driven work structures where people are given freedom in the way they work to deliver to desired or required business outcomes.

Hire good people and leave them alone. "

— WILLIAM MCKNIGHT, THEN CEO OF 3M, 1948

Restructures are without question a corporate reality today as merger and acquisition activity continues, although with reduced frequency in the post-GFC era of greater economic stability. However, there is no doubt organizations will continue to question their structures and resourcing based on future demands on them as a business. We are anticipating that while this kind of "top-down" approach to organizational and work design will continue, with the new world we are entering there may be more room for a bottom-up approach to work redesign. In this approach, those closest to the role requirements and organizational outputs will have an increased say in the way that their work gets done and how to deliver business objectives.

fuel
50

The knowledge worker

To the disruptive trends identified by the University of Phoenix Research Institute we would add the growth in the knowledge or service worker as discussed by Meister and Willyerd. They describe the rise of the knowledge worker who has to deal with an ever-increasing complexity of tasks. Some 70% of all jobs created in the US since 1998 have required a set of higher level conceptual skills, while transactional tasks have increasingly been streamlined, outsourced and restructured.

 The US Department of Education estimates that 60% of all new jobs in the twenty-first century will require skills that only 20% of current employees hold.

The importance of the knowledge worker who needs to be learning and career agile is evident today, and the engagement, retention and motivation of these knowledge workers will be vital to those organizations wanting to succeed in the 2020 workplace. The US Department of Education estimates that 60% of all new jobs in the twenty-first century will require skills that only 20% of current employees hold.

Given these disruptive forces, 10 skills (see next page) emerge as highly relevant to the productivity of the future workforce according to the University of Phoenix Research Institute and Institute for the Future.

THE CAREER-AGILE WORKER

We had the privilege recently of hearing Debra France of W.L. Gore & Associates (famous for their Gore-Tex product and in HR circles for their flat organization structure) describe a world where workers are already having to work in the ways described above by the University of Phoenix Research Institute. Gore-Tex is, and always has been, a passionately flat organization

SKILLS RELEVANT TO FUTURE WORKFORCE PRODUCTIVITY

- **Sense-making:** Being capable of getting to the deeper meaning or significance of what is being communicated.

- **Social intelligence:** Being capable of relating to others deeply and directly.

- **Novel, adaptive thinking:** Being capable of thinking and solution-generating outside of the norm to respond to unexpected and unique situations.

- **Cross-cultural competency:** being capable of operating in unfamiliar cultural settings, and utilizing differences for innovation.

- **Computational thinking:** Being capable of translating large amounts of data into useful abstract concepts, and to understand data-based reasoning.

- **New media literacy:** Being capable of leveraging new media forms to communicate persuasively.

- **Transdisciplinarity:** Being capable of understanding concepts across different disciplines to solve multi-faceted problems.

- **Design mindset:** Being capable of designing tasks, processes and work environments to help produce the outcomes we want.

- **Cognitive load management:** Being capable of filtering important information from the "noise," and using new tools to expand our mental functioning abilities.

- **Virtual collaboration:** Being capable of working productively with others across virtual distances.

by design, with not a single manager among the 10,000 employees. There are occasional leaders either temporarily or more permanently who are defined and chosen by their "followership." As Debra France describes

> When looking for someone to lead the People Function, it was put to the entire business: who would you follow in this organization in relation to People Leading practices? Who is doing things in the People space that you admire and who are making a difference in the way they work. From the employees' responses a "leader" is identified. More commonly in the Gore-Tex environment there are people who lead projects. The explanation from our history is "We manage projects not people. People manage themselves."

> We do have leaders, and those leaders are defined by followership. In other words — you are a leader when other people want to follow you. We have found that associates who use a coaching style for engaging associates generate great followership and end up becoming the most valued leaders.[4]

Debra posed the question to the Human Capital Institute summit conference in Florida in 2014:

> "Where do you think people get the better career development opportunity? In a flat organization with no leadership pathways at all or in a traditional hierarchical organization offering typical career ladder pathways?"

The resounding audience response was for the former and the reasons resonate with our view of a career-agile organization. Employees will be required to stretch and grow their skill-sets, to add more value to the business, to contribute more, to do so in a way that is visible and thought-leading to others, and that empowers others to also contribute their best towards a "purpose-aligned" project. Without doubt, the skills defined above by the University of Phoenix will be required, but there is equally a challenge to organizations to support the creation of career-agile employees to meet the needs of the future workplace.

Those of us born before the 1980s are the generations that will experience multiple careers, but the prospect is less certain for the Millennials who are entering the workforce today. This millennial generation is witnessing a major shift in employment dynamics, and the educated among them may have career experiences radically different from previous generations.

This generation, who increasingly will be knowledge or service workers, may witness the return of the lifetime employer, particularly with the organizations that have discovered what we call the "new lifestyle employment proposition."

With the advent of a talent shortage and dramatically shifting workplace demographics, employers are increasingly focused on talent retention. However, this seems to be a somewhat myopic reaction of trying to retain critical talent or high potentials, while the truly innovative organizations of our times are creating "lifestyle" or even lifetime employee models.

Organizations such as Facebook and Google are creating workplaces where work and life are so blurred that you can work day and night (or whenever you feel like it) but with every lifestyle need being catered to — whether it's roller-hockey interludes, ski holidays, access to gaming at work 24/7, or handling those other life considerations such as doctors, dentists, massage therapists and even a constant supply of great free food. Altogether, it results in every life need being catered for, from physical to social needs and beyond, meaning that your work can be your life.

Even the professional services firms such as Deloitte and PwC are critically aware of creating lifetime career paths for their employees. These traditional firms are creating alumni programs through social media, facilitating career breaks, and providing mentoring from the first career touch-point.

Mass career customization

Some of the professional services firms are even leading global thinking, such as with Deloitte's radical mass career customization (as described by Cathleen Benko and Anne Weisberg). In this approach, customized career propositions are presented to each employee, designed to retain talent over a lifetime, and allowing plenty of flex and stretch to provide ongoing challenge and opportunity, ensuring the retention of that employee over their lifetime.[5]

This practice is happening now, but the majority of organizations are still shortsightedly focused on compliance-based practices, restructuring and redundancies as short-term strategies to improve profitability and productivity.

 Meanwhile, the very smart organizations are stealthily focusing on unleashing individual productivity with flexible work practices that allow individuals to contribute day and night, to stay and play at work, to take career breaks, and return to productivity quickly.

Individualization of the employment proposition and meaningful work will be two key trends seen as we head towards the 2020 workplace.

ELEMENTS OF THE NEW LIFESTYLE CAREER PROPOSITION

- **Performance focused on productivity:** radical new performance measures are required based on output and trust.

- **Blurring of work and life:** ensuring great social connection at work that translates equally well across real and online worlds. Whether it is roller-hockey or ski weekends, the best firms are blurring these boundaries regularly, providing a social connection at work.

- **Leveraging social media to support connectivity:** this generation is being dubbed the "hyper-connected."[6] Embrace it and love it because this generation will work differently as a consequence, and we need to now switch our expectations for workplace behavior from compliance and attendance to productivity, creativity and performance. The Googles and Facebooks of this world have people so passionate about what they are doing that they work day and night.

- **And, most importantly, individualize the career proposition:** understand what is going to light the fire of each and every contributor and then look at what you need to do to enable that contribution. You need to understand the talents, motivators, values and career–lifestyle expectations of each employee and then tailor the career experience to meet each employee's unique wants and needs. Bersin by Deloitte, which provides some of the most valuable workplace analysis and futurist research, has indicated that "individualization" of the employment proposition and meaningful work will be two key trends we will witness as we head towards the 2020 workplace.[7]

This new "lifestyle" career proposition has a few essential ingredients for success.

BUILDING CAREER-AGILE ORGANIZATIONS

The world of work has changed quickly and is continuing to demand increased agility from people in all kinds of employment today. Organizations are increasingly having to prepare their people for working in this fast-changing environment. Career agility coaching is going to be part of the toolkit for HR to support people to meet current and future demands.

Increased globalization, flexible work practices and the hyper-connectivity resulting from the proliferation of social media are all putting increasing demands on workers and HR alike. This changing world of work is demanding different skills and behaviors from people, and not everyone is ready and able to respond to these changes.

The smart organizations are moving quickly to respond to this accelerating world. Dave Niekerk of Amazon describes the agility required of their people where everyone in the corporate support office has to spend time in the Fulfillment Center and where hundreds of new hires line up each week for orientation, are handed their laptops, given a rallying pep talk and then are expected to quickly find their way to contribute to the organization's effectiveness regardless of the role they have been hired into. Niekerk says if people working in the Fulfillment and Customer Service Centers are not "signing up" every day, they have the option of taking the money and running with their counter-intuitive "Pay to Quit" scheme. They want people who are committed every day to making a difference and who align with the business vision of everyone having an opportunity to do "meaningful work."[8]

A large number of organizations are struggling to compete with their own employee value propositions in response to the lifestyle proposition being offered by these leading companies. As talent shortages continue to loom ominously, other organizations will still need to retain talent and offer more flexible work practices to workers at all ages and stages to compete for fresh talent.

A trend noted in the engineering professional services sector particularly is the move to provide flexible work practices designed specifically to retain the older worker. Global research into career agility conducted by Fuel50, for example, showed that over 75% of all respondents aged 18 to 65 would prefer to work either a nine-day fortnight or a four-day week and would sacrifice salary to do so.

Tailoring an attractive employee proposition

In order to tailor an attractive employment proposition that supports agility in organizations it is important to understand the personal career wants and needs of each individual.

- What stage of their career are they at?

- How long have they been in their role?

- Do they want to "dial up or "dial down" their career right now?

- What other priorities do they have outside of work that they are trying to accommodate?

- How flexible are they in terms of location and place of employment?

By understanding each of these facets, a powerful conversation can be had with the individual to tailor their career experience, often at no cost to the organization at all (see Fig. 1.4). Career coaching is now incorporating diagnostics such as these, along with traditional career assessments like values, talents and interest inventories.

Developing a coaching culture

Building career agility through one-on-one coaching conversations is just the start. Leading organizations, such as Citigroup, Westpac Group, a Fortune 500 Global Bank, and Australian Best Employer 2012 winner Frucor, are layering individual coaching conversations with educating managers on how to have coaching conversations with their people. A layered approach works best, as sometimes this conversation is best delivered by someone else

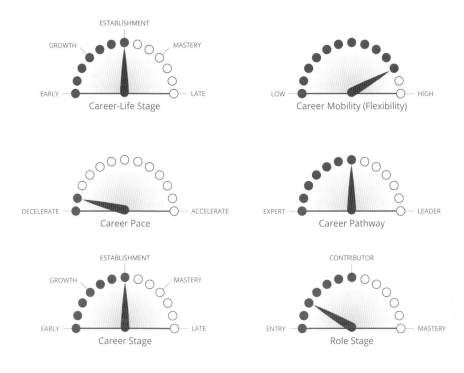

FIG 1.4

in the organization such as HR, a recruitment consultant or a mentor. So training additional people in the organization is an effective line of defense in the battle for talent and retention.

Jo Avenell, when General Manager of Human Resources at Westpac, built a coaching culture through a number of key initiatives, including developing and utilizing master coaches in their Coaching Academy to provide coaching for high potential employees. Jo says that "through the Coaching Academy our master coaches continuously develop their coaching capability, tangibly support the development of our talent and act as coaching role models for leaders in our talent pipeline."

In the words of one of our coaches: 'Some leaders succeed because they have charisma — the rest of us succeed because of coaching!'

— JO AVENELL

Debra France at W.L. Gore & Associates says, "You are a leader when other people want to follow you. We have found that associates who use a coaching style for engaging associates generate great followership and end up becoming the most valued leaders." She describes some of the factors that make their culture and extremely flat organizational style work. "It has always been known as our 'Lattice' organization where any associate can speak to any other associate." There is the bare minimum of levels, and "the little hierarchy we do have does not always imply authority: enterprise and division leaders are just as accountable for generating followership for their ideas as the newest team member."

If the first line of defense in creating an agile workforce is the coaching skills of your leaders, the second is in the education and support of your employees as well. Individual coaching workshops allow participants to learn about the changing world of work, understand the corporate environment, and appreciate their own personal values and drivers. An integral part of this type of workshop involves peer coaching support to help employees create and continue their own action plans to maintain agility.

Personal brand capital
A key concept covered in these coaching workshops is personal brand capital — and the increasing importance of personal reputation as we live in an increasingly social world. For example, people are being endorsed on LinkedIn, so those that don't even have a LinkedIn profile will be falling

behind the game. Meanwhile, others are publishing articles, contributing to thought-leading and building their reputation capital.

"Reputation capital will be the top currency in the 2020 workplace. This is the sum total of your personal brand, your expertise, and the breadth, depth and quality of your social networks. "

— MEISTER AND WILLYERD[9]

Meister and Willyerd in *The 2020 Workplace* assert that HR practitioners and coaches have a responsibility to prepare people for this world.

Career boot camps

Career agility coaching groups can be delivered in organizations by leveraging the recent sporting phenomenon of boot camps, which are proving to be highly effective in motivating people and maintaining peak fitness. Boot camp methods can be applied to creating career-agile employees by offering career boot camps that provide peer support, ongoing motivation, access to great career resources and tools, and which take coaching philosophies even further by providing resources so that these programs can be peer-led.

Career agility in employees is going to become an in-demand currency as organizations navigate towards the future workplace. Talent management will be a critical skill valued as an increasingly integral part of an organization's strategic planning, as agility in both the organization and its employees is increasingly demanded. As noted in *Harvard Business Review*, strategic planning cycles are becoming increasingly accelerated and are becoming more about agility, tactical planning and execution.[10]

NOTES

1   Retrieved from: www.slideshare.net/fred.zimny/future-work-skills2020.
2   Meister, J.C. and Willyerd, K. (2010). *The 2020 Workplace: How Innovative Companies Attract, Develop, and Keep Tomorrow's Employees Today*. Harper Business, New York, NY.
3   Ibid.
4   Retrieved from: www.debrafrance.com/blog.
5   Benko, C. and Weisberg, A. (2007). *Mass Career Customization: Aligning the Workplace with Today's Nontraditional Workforce*. Harvard Business Review Press, Boston, Massachusetts.
6   Meister, J.C. and Willyerd, K. (2010), op. cit.
7   Bersin by Deloitte (2014). HCI Employee Engagement Conference, 2014.
8   HRMI Conference, Newport Beach, July 2014.
9   Meister, J.C. and Willyerd, K. (2010), op. cit.
10 Blenko, M.W., Mankins, M.C. and Rogers, P. (2010). *Decide & Deliver: 5 Steps to Breakthrough Performance in Your Organization*. Harvard Business School Publishing, Boston, Massachusetts.

2 The Business Case for Retention

Across the globe, businesses are experiencing the retention challenge.

Carol Brown, when HRD for a global engineering services company, was faced with a lot of the organization's "knowledge capital" walking out the door as their valuable Baby Boomer "bubble" was approaching retirement, potentially leaving a significant skills and knowledge gap within the business.

Her driving need was to build a retention strategy for these workers that meant they were motivated to stay and work even past legal retirement and ensure knowledge transfer and business continuity while maintaining their personal lifestyle wants. These Baby Boomers, according to our Career Agility Trends Research,[1] are looking for micro tweaks in their working week to accommodate their golf, fishing, travel, grandchild care or whatever it is. They would happily stay employed and contributing, but with a reduced workload or working week.

At the other end of the spectrum we work with professional services firms that have invested in graduate talent who have been plied with attractive sign-on bonuses, late night drinking sessions and up-market meals as their "work-entry" experience. These same "expensive to sign" talent are then leaving in droves when they hit the 25 to 29-year-old mark. One law firm we worked with described this population as their most disengaged and most at risk of leaving.

Both these examples exemplify the retention business challenge that is being experienced across the globe and the need to craft individual retention plans to retain their valuable assets in an increasingly competitive talent landscape.

THE TALENT WARS ARE BACK ON

The global financial crisis gave us a reprieve. While McKinsey & Company were right to predict the talent wars as a critical business challenge of the new millennium, we have enjoyed a brief reprieve in the last five years, with hiring freezes and people clinging onto their jobs like barnacles.[2]

As the global economy emerges from the doldrums of the GFC, top business leaders and HR professionals alike have begun to formulate their battle plans. The talent wars have become a concrete reality, and the emerging picture from global labor market statistics confirms that they will become only more vicious and further entrenched.[3] While the reprieve may have lulled the more reactive HR practitioners into complacency, now more than ever the thaw is beginning to happen.[4] Developed economies, such as the US, are entering a new phase of economic stability, with reverberating consequences for both the labor market and HR practices at large. Growth is expected to pick up over 2014 and beyond, with emergent markets such as Latin America and China expected to spike in 2014, and dominant economies such as the US expected to spike between 2014 and 2018.[5] Talent mobility has now begun in earnest, with some predicting an exodus of talent as economies across the globe pick up.[6] However, the deep scars left by the dubious employment practices and mass layoffs of the crisis years have changed the labor market on a fundamental level. Pre-crisis employment tactics that focused predominantly on "capturing" top talent by fine-tuning recruitment strategies are no longer effective in this new period of talent-siege warfare.

The US labor market has now entered a period of relative stability since the turmoil created by the financial downfall in 2007/08. Voluntary turnover rates peaked in 2010, which was also a time when 22% of organizations

reported staff downsizing, 20% experienced a hiring freeze and 35% engaged in a restructure of their organization.[7]

The number of organizations reporting significant layoffs or employee downsizing dropped from 43% in 2010 to 21% in 2013. Urgency in making changes in major business practices has declined significantly, and broad changes in business strategy have steadily slowed, being replaced with a greater focus on execution. Even compensation practices are stabilizing, with only 18% making major adjustments, well below the 31% in 2010.[8]

As the global economy emerges from the doldrums of the GFC, top business leaders and HR professionals alike have begun to formulate their battle plans.

All around us, business confidence is growing. No longer do we have tales of mass layoffs, downsizing and financial scams on the pages of the *Financial Times*, and the images of protesters outside banks are a thing of the past. Statistics confirm that this new optimism is well-founded. For example, the UK economy grew by 1.9% in 2013, the highest level since 2007.[9] Predictions based on data from the US Department of Commerce foresee a 6.3% reduction in unemployment during 2014. At the same time, business spending is up 4.5–5% along with increased spending in key commercial markets as US growth strengthens.[10] Optimism has increased among small business, too, with an increase in both the number of new business start-ups and funding requests.[11] Overall, the US economy is expected to grow 2.7% in 2014.[12] Not surprisingly, this newfound business confidence is affecting employees themselves, who are now re-evaluating their current employment situation against a wealth of perceived opportunities elsewhere.

 Despite the forecasted shortage of talent in knowledge-based industries, job satisfaction indices have been in steady decline. In the last three years, job satisfaction has begun to trend downward, slowly slipping in the direction of the pre-recession rates.13 If this movement continues, employee turnover rates are likely to increase as employees now perceive an employment market that is more attractive to job seekers.[14]

Global trends in employee turnover

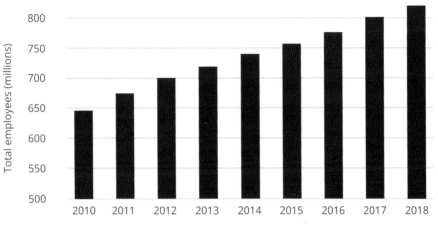

FIG 2.1   SOURCE: HAYGROUP (2014 A)

Percentage of employees satisfied with their position

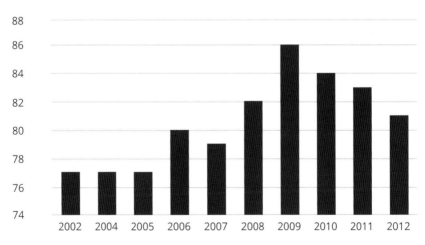

FIG 2.2   SOURCE: SOCIETY OF HUMAN RESOURCE MANAGEMENT (2012 B)

**As business confidence improves, people are
significantly more likely to begin researching
other opportunities, and they are willing to
take personal risks that they may not have
considered when the economic situation was
more challenging.**

A comparison between business and employment trends shows that as
business confidence is rising, there has also been a significant drop in job
satisfaction.[15] Job satisfaction refers to a cognitive judgment that employees
make regarding their overall satisfaction with their working conditions.
These judgments form the base against which they decide how much effort
to invest in their work and, ultimately, when to stay or go.[16] Not surprisingly,
these judgments are not formed in a vacuum, and are determined to a large
extent by surrounding economic conditions. Nowhere are these correlations
more apparent than in knowledge-based industries, where the wealth of
available opportunities is rapidly outstripping qualified labor supply.

According to US Department of Labor statistics for predicted labor market
trends for the year 2014, 39% of companies reported growth between 1%
and 10% in 2013. Furthermore, 81% of companies expect to add to their
staff in 2014, or remain at their current level, replacing people who leave.[17]
Knowledge-based professional industries added an average of 55,000 jobs
per month in 2013 in an otherwise fairly static employment market.[18]

THE TRUE COSTS OF ATTRITION ARE STAGGERING

In our everyday business conversations we are starting to hear about frightening attrition statistics. These statistics are increasingly entering executives' radar, with senior HR practitioners held accountable for these metrics. One contact center we have recently begun to work with reports a loss of 150 people per week. Furthermore, our own Fuel50 Career Agility Trends Research, published in 2013, [19] indicates that 60% of people intend to leave their organizations in the next three years. As replacing an employee is generally estimated to cost between one-half and five times that employee's annual salary, the cost to the organization of such churn is staggering.[20] Not to mention the time, skills and organizational know-how that walk out the door with employees.

RETENTION HAS BECOME CRITICAL

While the overall supply of qualified workers appears to exceed demand in a wide array of industries, jobs and locations, the match between viable candidates and open positions is, if anything, widening. Competition to attract and retain high-performing employees is therefore becoming increasingly fierce. While talent management programs were often among the first casualties of spending cuts imposed during the crisis years, the consequences of such short-sightedness have now become apparent.[21] The increase in viable employment opportunities for specialized workers amid a stable job market means that it is no longer sufficient to focus exclusively on attracting talent from an external talent pool that does not actually exist. The stalemate conditions brought by the new stability mean that retaining the talent within your ranks has now become the critical tactic to gain a competitive edge. Companies have now re-energized efforts to retain valued contributors, citing employee engagement and talent retention initiatives as a priority business objective and integral business strategy.[22]

> **Career development is paramount to a company's business strategy and is essential to ensuring that the company will have the people with the needed skills to meet client needs in a rapidly changing global world. Career development is also a key factor in attracting, retaining and engaging employees for increased productivity and satisfaction.**
> — MARY ANN BOPP OF IBM[23]

Some 65% of all organizations now budget for engagement initiatives and another 18% are considering formal budgets for it.[24]

SO WHY DO PEOPLE LEAVE?

In order to stem attrition, it is necessary to understand the underlying motives that cause employees to leave. Although the reasons for voluntary turnover are varied, our research has identified common threads that contribute to attrition across a variety of sectors. In most cases, attrition may be traced to the basic fact that employees leave because they feel that they are investing more in their work than they are receiving. This can occur due to a mismatch between the values, talents and working conditions, and, increasingly, lack of meaningful developmental and advancement opportunities. The combination of these factors determines engagement levels, job satisfaction and the overall value that employees place upon their job, which ultimately forms the basis of the decision of whether to stay or go.[25]

Both job satisfaction and engagement levels are strongly linked to turnover intentions and turnover rates, which they decrease up to 56%.[26]

Moving from strong disengagement to strong engagement decreases the probability of departure by 87%.[27]

MONEY CAN'T BUY YOU LOYALTY

Recent attrition trends confirm what savvy employers have long since known — money alone is no longer enough. In fact, research shows that when asked to estimate how satisfied they are with their current level of financial remuneration, disengaged employees respond they are dissatisfied, while engaged employees respond that they are satisfied, despite receiving exactly the same rate of compensation.[28] Salary increases and benefits have been found to be ineffective means to motivate and engage employees, with a growing number of both men and women expressing a preference for increased free time over wages.[29]

The results of a global study of 618 participants spanning 22 industries show that money and reimbursement did not feature as primary motivators for leaving. Rather, the primary determinants of attrition were career and job factors, followed by lack of career advancement opportunities at around three years of tenure.[30] This is especially true for the notoriously hard to motivate Generation Y employees, who respond to developmental and growth opportunities where monetary incentives fail.[31]

Career and job factors have been shown to be key determinants of reported engagement levels, and these were shown to determine 59% of overall attrition.[32]

Employees who strongly agreed that *"There is someone at work who encourages my development"* and *"In the last six months, someone at work has talked to me about my progress"* **were twice as likely to be engaged, and 92% intended to stay with their companies for at least another year.**[33]

PERSON–JOB FIT

Not surprisingly, statistics show that much attrition is also due to a mismatch between personal talents and role requirements, as well as missed expectations relating to working conditions, which determine up to 59% of attrition at least within the first year of tenure.[34] Perceived fit between the employee and the flexibility of working conditions was found to be associated with increased engagement, especially for workers over 45.[35] On the other hand, perceived misfit between personal capabilities and role requirements significantly increases stress and job strain, as employees perceive themselves poorly equipped to face the demands of their roles on a daily basis.[36] The results of one global study found that 52% of overall attrition occurs in the first year of employment, due to "poor fit between individual and organizational values" (37%) and "missed expectations of duties/or schedule" (30%). Interestingly, "lack of direct possibilities for advancement" predicted only 12% of first year attrition, underscoring the importance of values-based personal factors in determining early attrition rates.[37]

Some 54% of all subsequent attrition occurs at around three years of tenure, largely due to "lack of career advancement opportunities" (50%). However, it is too late at this point to begin career discussions that could have assisted in managing expectations and providing appropriate development opportunities. Such discussions need to begin as early as the recruitment phase.[38]

 Some 54% of all subsequent attrition occurs at around three years of tenure, largely due to "lack of career advancement opportunities" (50%).

Tailoring working conditions

Given that most employees leave because their employment conditions correspond poorly to their personal needs and career objectives, any attempt to tailor working conditions to the preferences of the individual employee will increase the value that the employee places on their current job. This, in turn, increases satisfaction and engagement levels and reduces voluntary turnover.[39]

With retention such an issue and the talent wars back in earnest, there is increasing competition for talent once again. We are hearing more of talent poaching, particularly of key or critical talent. It is now a necessity for organizations to build compelling retention plans for their people. The only way to do that is to ensure that you have a customized career proposition for every employee, or at least for those that are identified as critical talent to the business.

Mary Ann Bopp, IBM's Head of Career Development, describes the situation eloquently:

> *"Business priorities determine the human capital requirements, including the learning and career development strategies. To get the desired business results the organization must identify the needed knowledge and skills, determine expertise levels and gaps and create and implement a career development strategy for achieving the required levels of capabilities needed.* **Career development thus becomes the essential driver of bottom line results."**

NOTES

1 Fuel50 (2013). *Career Agility Trends Research*.
   Retrieved from: www.fuel50.com/research/agility

2 Ibid.

3 The "War for Talent" was first identified by McKinsey & Company, in 1996. For a more recent review see Beechler, S. and Woodward, I.C. (2009). The global "war for talent". *Journal of International Management*, 15, 273–85.

4 See Chambers, E.G., Foulon, M., Handfield-Jones, H., Hankin, S.M. and Michaels, E.G. (1998). The war for talent. *The McKinsey Quarterly*, 3, 44–57.

5 HayGroup (2014a). *Preparing for Take-off*. Retrieved from: http://atrium.haygroup. com/downloads/marketingps/ww/Preparing%20for%20take%20off%20-%20 executive%20summary.pdf.

6 *New York Times*, March 8, 2014.

7 These statistics were released by the US Bureau of Labor, and were published in *Talentkeepers Global Talent and Retention Report 2013*. Retrieved from: www. talentkeepers.com/download/2013-TalentKeepers-Employee-Engagement-Retention-Trends-Report-Final.pdf.

8 *Talentkeepers Global Talent and Retention Report 2013*. Retrieved from: www. talentkeepers.com/download/2013-TalentKeepers-Employee-Engagement-Retention-Trends-Report-Final.pdf.

9 BBC Business News Report, January 28, 2014.

10 Payne, D. (2014). *Kiplingers' Economic Outlooks, March 2014*. Retrieved from: www. kiplinger.com/tool/business/T019-S000-kiplinger-s-economic-outlooks/.

11 NFIB, 2014, see NFIB Research Foundation (2014).

12 This statistic was published in a Kiplinger Economic Outlooks report based on Statistics from the US Bureau of Labor; see Payne, D. (2014). *Kiplingers' Economic Outlooks, March 2014*. Retrieved from: www.kiplinger.com/tool/business/T019-S000-kiplinger-s-economic-outlooks/.

13 *Talentkeepers Global Talent and Retention Report 2013*. Retrieved from: www. talentkeepers.com/download/2013-TalentKeepers-Employee-Engagement-Retention-Trends-Report-Final.pdf.

14 Society of Human Resource Management (2014). *Tracking Trends in Employee Turnover*. Retrieved from: www.shrm.org/Research/benchmarks/Documents/ Trends%20in%20Turnover_FINAL.pdf.

15 See Schaufeli, W.B. and Bakker, A.B. (2004b). Job demands, job resources, and their relationship with burnout and engagement: A multi-sample study. *Journal of Organizational Behavior*, 25(3), 293–315; Harter, J.K., Schmidt, F.L. and Hayes, T.L. (2002). Business-unit level relationship between employee satisfaction, employee engagement, and business outcomes: A meta-analysis. *Journal of Applied Psychology*, 87, 268–79; Benson, G.S. (2006). Employee development, commitment and intention to turnover: a test of "employability" policies in action. *Human Resource Management Journal*, 16(2), 173–92.

16 Society of Human Resource Management (2012b). *2012 Employee Job Satisfaction and Engagement: How Employees are Dealing with Uncertainty*. SHRM, Alexandria, Virginia.

17 These statistics were published by US Department of Labor (2014) and published in *Talentkeepers Global Talent and Retention Report 2013*. Retrieved from: www. talentkeepers.com/download/2013-TalentKeepers-Employee-Engagement-Retention-Trends-Report-Final.pdf.

18 US Department of Labor, Bureau of Statistics (2014b).*Turnover and Job Openings Statistics Report February 2014*. Retrieved from: www.bls.gov/news.release/pdf/jolts. pdf; Harter, J.K., Schmidt, F.L. and Hayes, T.L. (2002). Business-unit level relationship between employee satisfaction, employee engagement, and business outcomes: A meta-analysis. *Journal of Applied Psychology*, 87, 268–79.

19 Fuel50 (2013), op. cit.

20 Robinson, J. (May 8, 2008). Turning around employee turnover. *The Gallup Business Journal.* Retrieved from: http://businessjournal.gallup.com/content/106912/turning-

around-your-turnover-problem.aspx#3.

21 Benko, C. and Weisberg, A. (2007). *Mass Career Customization: Aligning the Workplace with Today's Nontraditional Workforce*. Harvard Business Review Press, Boston, Massachusetts.

22 *Pulse on Leaders* (February 19, 2009). Personnel Decisions International (Press release); Benko and Weisberg (2007), op. cit.

23 Bopp, M., Bing, D. and Forte-Trammell, S. (2007). *Agile Career Development, Lessons and Approaches from IBM*. IBM Press.

24 *Pulse on Leaders* (February 19, 2009). Personnel Decisions International (Press release).

25 See *Talentkeepers Global Talent and Retention Report 2013*. Retrieved from: www.talentkeepers.com/download/2013-TalentKeepers-Employee-Engagement-Retention-Trends-Report-Final.pdf.

26 Schaufeli and Bakker (2004b), op. cit. *Talentkeepers Global Talent and Retention Report 2013*. Retrieved from: www.talentkeepers.com/download/2013-TalentKeepers-Employee-Engagement-Retention-Trends-Report-Final.pdf.

27 Schaufeli and Bakker (2004b), op. cit.

28 *Talentkeepers Global Talent and Retention Report 2013*. Retrieved from: www.talentkeepers.com/download/2013-TalentKeepers-Employee-Engagement-Retention-Trends-Report-Final.pdf.

29 Gallup Institute (2013). *State of the American Workplace: Employee engagement insights for US business leaders*. Retrieved from: www.gallup.com/strategicconsulting/163007/state-american-workplace.aspx.

30 *Talentkeepers Global Talent and Retention Report 2013*. Retrieved from: www.talentkeepers.com/download/2013-TalentKeepers-Employee-Engagement-Retention-Trends-Report-Final.pdf.

31 Benko, C. and Anderson, M. (2010). *The Corporate Lattice: Achieving High Performance in the Changing World of Work*. Harvard Business Review Press, Boston, Massachusetts.

32 These figures were published in a report by Talentkeepers (2013, op. cit.). These characteristics of Generation Y employees have been independently observed by a number of thought leaders, including Benko and Weisberg (2007, op. cit.); The Gallup Institute (2008).

33 The Gallup Institute (2008).

34 Robinson, J. (May 8, 2008). Turning around employee turnover. *The Gallup Business Journal*. Retrieved from: http://businessjournal.gallup.com/content/106912/turning-around-your-turnover-problem.aspx#3.

35 Pitt-Catsouphes, M. and Matz-Costa, C. (2008). The multi-generational workforce: Workplace flexibility and engagement. *Community, Work & Family*, 11, 215–29.

36 Lazarus, R.S. and Folkman, S. (1984). *Stress, Appraisal, and Coping*. Springer, New York, NY; Schaufeli and Bakker (2004a), op. cit.

37 *Talentkeepers Global Talent and Retention Report 2013*, op. cit. For an overview of talent management practices that stress the use of personal talents and workplace factors with case studies see Glen, C. (2006). Key skills retention and motivation: the war for talent still rages and retention is the high ground. *Industrial and Commercial Training*, 38(1), 37–45. See also Westerman, J.W. and Vanka, S. (2005). A cross-cultural empirical analysis of person-organization fit measures as predictors of student performance in business education: Comparing students in the United States and India. *Academy of Management Learning & Education*, 4(4), 409–20.

38 *Talentkeepers Global Talent and Retention Report 2013,* op. cit.

39 For empirical papers in support of the links between personalized work conditions, engagement satisfaction and turnover see Harter et al. (2002); Bhatnagar (2007); Schaufeli and Bakker (2004a); Tims and Bakker (2010); Tims, Bakker and Derks (2013); Sonnentag et al. (2012); Van Rooy et al. (2011); Bakker, Demerouti and Sanz-Vergel (2014).

3 | The Business Case for Career Engagement

Why you actually kind of have to "do career development"

TALENT-DRAG OR TALENT-LIFT: WHAT WOULD YOU RATHER HAVE?

Chatting to my hairdresser Brian the other week, we got talking about the kind of employees you really want on the team. I was complimenting him on a staff member, Amanda, who had stepped up lately and was a delight to deal with, to the extent that I would happily trust her with my very high maintenance hair, if Brian was ever to be unavailable — and this is high praise from me because I am fussy!

Brian described both what I would term "drag" and "lift" employees. He went on to describe another employee as "hard work," "high maintenance," and not adding a lot of value. He said she was away having elective surgery this week (I wondered but didn't ask!) and he relayed how earlier in the day another client had quipped, "Well, I hope it helps her move a bit faster!" Classic "Talent-Drag" employee! And it's really not a good sign when your clients notice these things.

On the other hand, Amanda was clearly a "lift" employee: she was adding incredible value, engaging with clientele, using her initiative and was a pleasure to deal with at all times. She was absolutely *lifting* the morale of the team, the atmosphere in the salon and even the performance of the business.

Brian had just hired a second new employee, Ben, even though he had just filled a vacant position, because of Ben's positive spark, personality, willingness to work hard and add value. This young man's father had been a barber and Ben had decided that he wanted to be involved in the trade, had researched exactly what salon he wanted to work for and the kind of person he wanted to learn from. He really knew what he wanted and had impressed Brian with his research and great attitude. Ben has all the makings of a "lift" employee.

ENGAGED EMPLOYEES

What we are really talking about here are *engaged* employees. Engaged employees bring their passions to work, know what values are important to them and are aware of what skills and talents they want to contribute and to develop further. You as a manager can then get insight into how to get that spark of engagement alive and well in all of your employees, not just those who have what I call the natural "lift" effect. It is possible to reduce the "drag" factor and increase the "lift" across an entire team and business.

 Engaged employees can triple the productivity and profitability of a business, and they are just generally great to have on the team.[1]

The dangers of disengagement

As we see from the story above, there is a clear performance differential between the engaged and the disengaged person at work. Every business has significant untapped potential in its workforce, whether small or large. Across the globe, there is a ratio of six engaged to four disengaged, but in the US the problem is even more significant with a concerning seven disengaged employees to every three engaged employees. And of the seven disengaged, two are actively disengaged, meaning that organization sabotage and damage to your brand are real threats. What are these people going to say to your customers or do to your product? This 2013 data shows that US organizations still have a lot of work to be done to improve engagement in their business.

Active disengagement is costing the US an estimated $450 billion each year in lost productivity and other costs.[2]

Untapped potential

In our global Career Agility Trends Research in 2013, we saw that 75% of employees actually want to contribute more at work. They want to bring more of their talents to work and use more of their skills.[3] What this means for you as an organization is that you have untapped potential sitting within your business. If each employee contributes just a little bit more, or adds just a little bit more value to their team's goals and outcomes, you are achieving the aspirational ideal of discretionary effort. And discretionary effort is the basis of engagement (as we will show at the end of this chapter).

Untapped potential
There is a higher ratio of engaged to actively
disengaged employees throughout the US

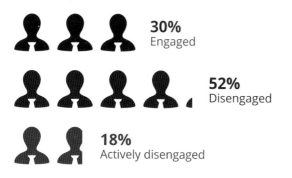

30%
Engaged

52%
Disengaged

18%
Actively disengaged

FIG 3.1   SOURCE: GALLUP (2013)

THE STRONG BUSINESS CASE FOR ENGAGEMENT

If you can shift the ratio of engaged to disengaged employees in your
business you can expect significant business gains. Engagement can make a
huge difference to the performance of a business. There is consistent strong
evidence now to show the link between engagement and profitability and
performance of a business. You can expect up to 150 times the shareholder
return in an organization where you have a ratio of nine engaged to one
disengaged employees. And where you only have a ratio of two engaged
to one disengaged you are more likely to see an average of 2% loss to
shareholders. If organizations can increase the proportion of engaged to
disengaged employees at work you will see clear business benefits.

The business case for engagement is strong

When you have an engaged workforce you will have better customer service, better quality and more innovation. What's more, Gallup in 2014 showed that engagement positively impacts productivity, performance, profitability and customer loyalty and negatively impacts absenteeism and employee turnover.[4] So we know that engagement delivers business benefit. Clearly. So how do we get it?

 ## Three times the innovation will occur in organizations with high engagement.[5]

+147% higher earning per share

Untapped potential
Organisations with an average of 9.3 engaged employees for every actively disengaged employee in 2010–2011 experienced 147% higher earning per share compared with their competition in 2011–2012.

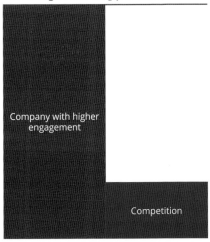

Company with higher engagement

Competition

FIG 3.2   SOURCE: GALLUP (2013)

DRIVERS OF ENGAGEMENT

Career opportunities

According to Aon Hewitt research, across the globe the top driver of engagement is career opportunities (see Fig. 3.3).[6] It is consistently rated everywhere as the number one driver, and this trend has been seen year after year. Moreover, this is increasing rather than shrinking, with a 3% increase of this factor as a driver of engagement in the last 12 months to July 2014.

	2011 (Global)	2012 (Global)	2013 (Global)	Asia Pacific	Europe	Latin America	North America
Career Opportunities	1	1	1	1	1	1	1
Organisation Reputation	3	2	3		2		3
Pay		3	4	2	3	4	
Recognition	2	4		4		2	5
Communication	4	5	5			3	
Managing Performance	5		2	5	5		2
Innovation					4		
Brand alignment				3		5	4

FIG 3.3   SOURCE: AON HEWITT (2014)

A deeper dive into the drivers of engagement shows that of the top six drivers of engagement, three are directly related to career engagement, as highlighted in the pathway to engagement diagram below, and a fourth is indirectly related to career engagement.

Top drivers of engagement
Four of the top six drivers of engagement are career related.

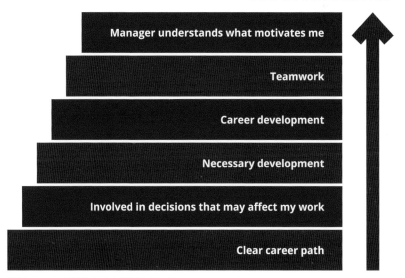

FIG 3.4   SOURCE: AON HEWITT (2013)

Visible career pathway

Having a clear line of sight to a career pathway is important to people. Your staff need to know:

- That they have career growth opportunities within their organization

- Where to find those opportunities

- How other people have succeeded in those pathways

- What the steps are to take them towards their aspirational roles.

When people can see how they can grow their career with you, they are more motivated to put in the effort and grow skills and competencies that will drive your business forward.

This is where your communication of pathways is vital. Many organizations struggle to communicate the career success stories and pathway opportunities for people in a simple, effective way. The best-practice organizations are now using technology enablers that are emerging on the market to help them communicate their career pathway proposition in a way that is visible to all employees. We are increasingly seeing organizations invest in either buying or building in-house tools that will enable them to provide this information to employees. And for good reason, too.

Receiving development necessary for role

The second driver identified by Aon Hewitt was being given the necessary development for their role. This means people are given the right skills and training to deliver to their role requirements. Most organizations make an effort to ensure that people do get the necessary development for their work. But in organizations where this is not done consistently you risk impacting engagement and productivity negatively. People feel disenchanted if left to their own devices and not given the support to deliver to their job requirements.

Career development

Moving further up the ladder towards engagement, we see that once the hygiene factor of being given the immediately necessary skills for their work tasks is taken care of, career development is highly valued by employees. You can build a stronger organizational commitment where organization and employees have mutual dedication to development. Mary Ann Bopp of IBM, co-author of *Agile Career Development*, describes this as a joint venture. There is a stronger sense of quid pro quo. "You provide me with career growth and I will be more committed and work harder for you!" Quite simple.

Employees are willing to give a lot to their organizations, but in these times, they also need to know that there is also a return on investment for them personally. "What's in it for me?" (WIFM) is a valid question for employees to ask. There has been a shift in the balance of power in organizations in recent times, and that balance has shifted to the employees. This is something we are likely to see shift even further still as the GFC impact recedes and we experience the big thaw in the talent freeze that organizations had in place during the tough economic times.

"You do this for me and I will be more committed and work harder for you!" Quite simple.

What we need to do right now is build a stronger psychological contract with our employees to achieve more "sticky" employees and gain the desired engagement and discretionary effort benefits. Committing to building the career capital and personal marketability of your employees will deliver a stronger commitment and loyalty to your organization. What it really comes down to is:

- "Why would I leave you if I can grow my career here with you?"

- "If I am better off with you, why would I look elsewhere?"

- "If you are investing in me, and I am better off as a consequence, why would I move on right now?"

There are lots of organizations who are getting this right increasingly, and their employment brands and reputations are becoming stronger as a consequence. All the graduates can typically tell you which of the law or accounting firms will give them the best career prospects. They don't need publicity pieces or business rankings to tell them. They know it from their friends and colleagues who are a few steps ahead of them; it is talked about all the time. This is true of so many industries. The businesses that are doing a good job of employment branding and providing a great career proposition get talked about. All the time! We are probably all equally tired of hearing about Google and its intern experience. There has even been a movie about it, for goodness' sake.

Creating a great career proposition for your employees and investing in their career development has significant pay-offs in terms of your employment brand and employee value proposition. It is our belief that those businesses with the strongest employment brands are the ones doing the best job of building what we call the career value proposition (CVP). This is truly the WIFM for your people and prospective hires.

Having a manager who understands motivation

Looking back at our step ladder to engagement (Fig. 3.4), the last factor is "having a manager who understands what motivates me." We have included this as part of the career proposition, because in our experience this is the essence of an effective, powerful career conversation between an employee and their manager. It is the heart of the employee–manager relationship. If a manager can get insight into the career drivers and motivators of each of their employees, they have the opportunity to tap into the "discretionary effort" that delivers engagement. If my manager understands what my personal drivers are, what I most love to do at work, and creates even small (but hopefully) regular opportunities to do these activities at work, there is no question that my personal motivation and engagement will lift.

 Each of us has individual talents and interests that are unique. We will feel most aligned, committed and satisfied at work when we have a chance to use those skills and talents at work.

A global career trends survey highlighted that 81% of people are not fully utilizing their talents at work. They feel they have more to contribute.[7] A staggering 75% of people reported that they actually wanted to do more to contribute to their businesses.[8] Again, this is significant untapped potential sitting within your organization — if you can just find out what those talents and motivations are. Even better, if you can give your managers insight into what will engage and motivate each employee, you will have instant access to increased productivity and engagement.

Some 81% of employees report that they are not fully utilizing their talents at work.

Discretionary effort

Over 50% of Millennials believe they can add more value to their employers according to Fuel50's Career Agility Trends Research (2013). This is an opportunity to tap into discretionary effort which has long been shown to link with productivity and profitability,[9] if you can just understand what the contributions these Millennials are keen to make.

Work responsibilities and demands comparison

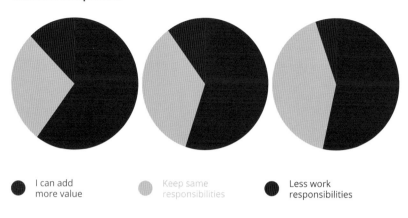

I can add more value

Keep same responsibilities

Less work responsibilities

FIG 3.5   SOURCE: FUEL50 (2013)

THE IMPORTANCE OF CAREER DEVELOPMENT

There is no question that career development is a valuable contributor to organizational performance and will be a key determinant of your engagement. Sixty-five percent of all organizations now budget for engagement initiatives and another 18% are considering formal budgets for it.[10]

Organizations that are communicating an individualized career proposition to their people will have a far greater chance of retaining and engaging their employees. They will also be effective in creating the career agility within their workforce that will be a contributor to future business success in a competitive landscape. In the next chapters we will share some of the key tactics that can be utilized to deliver customized career propositions. These propositions will bring the engagement, performance and retention outcomes that will create a competitive business advantage.

NOTES

1   Deloitte (2013).
2   Aon Hewitt (2013).
3   Fuel50 (2013). *Career Agility Trends Research*.
    Retrieved from: www.fuel50.com/research/agility
4   Gallup Institute (2014). *State of the American Workplace: Employee engagement insights for US business leaders*. Retrieved from: www.gallup.com/ strategicconsulting/163007/state-american-workplace.aspx.
5   Deloitte (2013).
6   Aon Hewitt (2014).
7   Fuel50 (2013), op. cit.
8   Ibid.
9   Aon Hewitt (2011).
10 *Pulse on Leaders* (February 19, 2009). Personnel Decisions International (Press release).

The Business Case for Leader Enablement

4

And organizational commitment to a career engagement best practice model

Career development needs to be individually driven, manager enabled and organizationally supported.[1]

LEADERS ARE CRITICAL TO CAREER ENGAGEMENT

Not so long ago, a leader we were working with returned to work from a one-day off-site training program in how to deliver a powerful career conversation. He found a resignation letter from a valued team member. He immediately decided he needed to put theory into practice and asked the team member to consider reflecting on their career values and aspirations more thoroughly before he would accept the resignation. The manager then sat down with our Fuel 50 *Career Insights* report the following day and delivered a powerful coaching conversation. It turned around the situation so effectively that the team member concerned is now a highly valued contributing general manager in that business.

Without question, leaders are critical to a best-practice career engagement strategy. Yet, we find that many leaders are fearful of career conversations, and many HR practitioners are anxious that leaders are not well-equipped to deliver these conversations in a meaningful and powerful way.

Communication is key

Communication is where engagement all starts. Effective two-way communication is directly linked to increased engagement by a number of mechanisms. At a fundamental level, effective communication improves leadership at all levels of the organization by fostering rapport between managers and their reports.

Effective leadership is the lifeblood of all organizations and the most effective leaders contribute to the career growth of their direct reports. As we will expand on in Part 3 of this book, career development needs to be individually driven, manager enabled and organizationally supported.[2] Clearly, this can only occur effectively if information flows in an efficient, open and two-way manner. Under this framework, the spotlight comes to rest upon the manager, who emerges as the enabler and facilitator holding the key to the career success of their reports.

By leveraging the transformative power of communication supported by relevant career insights, leaders can increase their effectiveness exponentially. An effective manager is also a primary determinant of both engagement and attrition, as it is common knowledge that "people do not quit their jobs, they quit their managers."

Leader–member exchange

At the root of contemporary research into the psychology of leader effectiveness lies a concept known as leader–member exchange (LMX). At its essence, it is the *frequency* and *quality* of interactions between leaders and their team members.[3] While early studies sought to identify successful leadership as the result of specific behaviors that the leader exhibits as an individual, more recent research has realized the futility of such an approach. Ultimately, successful leadership is the upshot of a successful *interchange* between leaders and their direct reports, and communication is the vital link that allows this to occur. Better communication leads to better quality relationships between leaders and their team members irrespective of organizational context. Scientific studies show the simple LMX is one of the most powerful and reliable predictors of leader effectiveness, which it has been shown to predict by up to 37%.[4]

 It is our view that the effectiveness of leader–team member exchanges can be dramatically impacted when leaders have insight into the core career motivators, values and motivated talents of each of their direct reports.

IF YOU DON'T KNOW IT'S BROKEN, HOW CAN YOU FIX IT?

The importance of an active approach to leadership based on regular joint goal-setting, and appropriate feedback, is generally accepted within management circles as basic to effective management. However, strangely, it is only now being extended as an effective approach to tackling staff engagement and retention issues. Many leaders within organizations will tend towards the "business as usual" approach, and you assume that everything is going well until you realize with a jolt that it is not, because you are faced with a recruiting challenge when a number of your staff indicate intention to leave. When some staff begin to leave, you can rest assured that others will as well. Unfortunately, employees are at least to some extent like lemmings — seeing one colleague leave will often provoke a re-evaluation of their satisfaction with their current roles, causing them to find fault where none previously existed. This in turn is linked to decreased job satisfaction and increased turnover intention.

In many cases, drops in employee satisfaction can be easily prevented, if you go about it with the right attitude. Employees weigh their decisions regarding the amount of energy they exert in their current roles against the relative benefits they receive in compensation. These value judgments are not static, however, just as job satisfaction is not something that is determined by the stipulated conditions one agrees to when signing the employment contract.

 Job satisfaction is the sum of the many and often subconscious value judgments that employees are constantly forming about their working conditions as they sign up for work each morning.

It is these judgments that determine the amount of effort employees are willing to invest in their work, and they also form the basis of decisions regarding when to stay and when to go.

Research shows that even small inconveniences, known as "daily hassles," can have a huge impact on these value judgments that determine employee satisfaction. In fact, these daily inconveniences are a fundamental determinant of overall engagement levels.[5]

Enabling growth and performance

Collaborative work shaping is required to proactively problem-solve around these daily work hassles. This will mean employees are more effectively enabled to deliver on their work objectives and gain personal satisfaction while also being enabled to extend their skills and contributions, thus adding to their personal career capital.

> **There are many examples of leaders who see that their primary job as leaders is to "remove blockers" and "enable the growth and performance of their team members."**

These effects can be magnified exponentially if leaders can learn to apply some simple techniques to allow them to understand their team members as individuals on a deeper level. Nowhere is this truer than during career conversations, which provide a perfect opportunity to broach these subjects, to show an interest in your team, and to discuss important questions fundamental to your working relationship. In most organizations

fuel 50

the performance review has formed the traditional setting for more intimate discussions between managers and their team members. However, there are a number of reasons why this does not work.

WHY PERFORMANCE APPRAISALS ARE NOT ENOUGH

The performance review has always been constructed around the idea of judgment. In its traditional form, the performance review provides a formalized occasion for the manager to provide feedback on the net sum of the offerings that the employee has brought to the table with reference to some often unspecified performance expectation. In many cases, these reviews represent the only setting in which the employee may have the ear of their manager. Also, tragically, in many organizations they may be the only circumstances in which employees receive feedback on how they are doing. Most of us who have had a performance review ourselves, or who have friends or colleagues working in the corporate world, will have noticed that these occasions are generally met with a considerable degree of anxiety and apprehension, mixed with the desire to actually know how we are doing and how we have "performed."

While the performance review is in many ways a necessary evil, it is not the forum in which to enhance leader–team member rapport, and in which to ask those more personal questions which tend to get swept under the carpet amid the flurry of "business as usual" activity. The communication is predominantly one-sided; the manager pronounces judgment and the employee listens and explains. Unfortunately, the nature of performance reviews is that they tend to minimize the positive and accentuate the negative, a sure recipe for disengagement!

Negative (aka "constructive") feedback during appraisals is considered by many a necessary evil to improve performance. However, it is fundamentally incompatible with a conversation designed to encourage employees to open up and to share their personal aspirations and circumstances with their manager. Evaluative threat, which is exactly what your team member is faced with during a performance review, is one of the most powerful ways to induce a stress reaction.[6] Even if the employee has performed poorly and knows it, telling them so in a performance review will not miraculously increase engagement or improve performance.

Talent actualization

Development conversations focused on talent actualization are the answers to unlocking potential and accelerating both engagement and performance. With objective data insights on individual talents, motivators and engagers, it is possible for all leaders to tap into the full potential that exists in their teams. **Not only customizing a career proposition to meet different group needs, but across all employees, we seek to create individual actualization.** This is the new engagement proposition.

Creating individual actualization is the new engagement proposition.

LEADER ENABLEMENT

This new engagement proposition has already been validated across hundreds of organizations around the globe. Leader career management practices are seen as a key factor affecting a range of HR metrics, such as absenteeism and employee turnover, and they are directly linked to overall organizational financial performance and revenue per employee.[7]

Improving leader effectiveness

One of the key ways in which career management practices benefit organizations is by improving leader effectiveness. Leaders are the touch-point between employees and their organization, and a shift in the quality of the leader–employee relationship is the most effective means to drive engagement. Not surprisingly, the majority of our client organizations

(57%) recognize the need to ensure a consistently high level of leader effectiveness by formally training their leaders to have more effective career conversations.[8] Despite these investments in leader training, only 11% of respondents surveyed were able to say with confidence that they track to see whether career conversations are actually happening. Leaders did not hold career conversations with all team members in 43% of responding organizations. This is unsurprising given that team member development was included as a criterion for assessing leadership performance in only 60% of organizations. In those organizations in which career conversations were happening, respondents expressed concern regarding both the quality and the frequency of these discussions.

The overwhelming majority of HR respondents reported that leaders were not confident in their coaching skills, suggesting that lack of perceived ability can be a major barrier to implementing career management practices and ensuring that they actually occur. Despite the fact that most respondents offered career coaching to all employees and not just top performers, 32% responded that leaders do not actually have these conversations with all team members. This underscores the need to ensure that theory is effectively translated into practice by tracking and recording the impact of career management practices against objective criteria.

Identifying the developmental needs of their team and formulating strategies to address these emerged as the most important areas for leader improvement overall.

 One simple way to achieve leader effectiveness is by including staff development outcomes as an index for evaluating leader performance, a practice carried out by 40% of respondents.

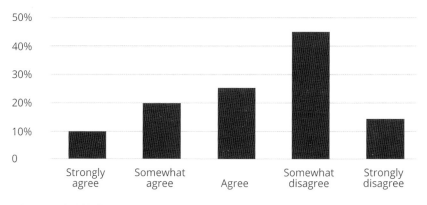

Managers are confident in their coaching skills

FIG 4.1   SOURCE: CRAWLEY & FULTON (2014)

IMPROVING ORGANIZATIONAL EFFECTIVENESS

Most organizations perceive career management to be a partnership between the employee and manager, supported by an enabling organizational framework. They back this up with solid talent management practices, including recruiting internally where possible (89%) and formally integrating flexible working practices within their organization (68%). Survey results were more varied regarding higher level career management practices, however. Despite the fact that flexible working practices were possible in most organizations, career breaks were *not acceptable* in 30% of organizations, and making use of flexible working practices was felt to jeopardize chances of promotion by over 30% of respondents. These results underscore the need for cultural change in many organizations, including promotion of a safe and diversity-friendly climate and ensuring senior management acceptance of career management processes.

At an organizational level, a few key areas emerged which separated top performing organizations from their competitors. These include:

- Sculpting attractive high status expert career paths in addition to the classic managerial roles

- Crafting a definition of "talent" that is not limited to the capacity to move up the organizational ladder

- Offering developmental opportunities above and beyond those required for current role performance.

Importance of time

Improved communication remains a sticking point within many organizations, especially regarding the accessibility to roles that become available. Some 24% of organizations responded that their managers were not aware of the career ambitions of their direct reports, while 43% were not aware of how their current talent resources aligned with organizational strategy. Reasons for these difficulties include lack of oversight regarding the talents within their team and, critically, lack of time. Some 48% of organizations reported that managers lacked time to support the career growth of their direct reports.

 Time is the most valuable resource that leaders have to offer, and careful planning that allows employees to come to career conversations well prepared is critical to ensure efficiency and maximum impact.

Initial analysis of our benchmarking survey results strongly supports the effectiveness of optimal career management practices as a means to improve objective business outcomes. Our data suggest that increased HR effectiveness as a result of effective career management practices corresponds to improved overall financial performance at an organizational level.

- Businesses who had a higher career management practices score reported significant increase in overall revenue growth ($r = .312$, $p < .01$).

- This was correlated to increased revenue per employee (r = .394, p < .01), suggesting that this effect is likely due to increased efficiency and discretionary effort among employees as opposed to change in external market conditions.

A closer examination of the performance outcome metrics indicates that improved career management practices appear to improve HR performance via a number of channels.[9]

- Improved career management practices help in generating sufficient talent to meet strategic business objectives, which corresponded to the ability to fill key leadership positions internally (r = .328, p < .01) and decreased recruitment costs (r = .221, p < .05).

- Career development practices typical of lattice organizations such as lateral moves further improved financial outcomes via decreased voluntary attrition (r = -.225, p < .05). This was linked to increased revenue per employee (r = .224, p < .04) and increased overall revenue growth (r = .241, p < .05).

- Top performing organizations in terms of career management tended to do so across the board, reporting better overall HR and business performance ($F_{(4,63)}$ = 3.61, p = .01, Np2 = .18).

(Crawley and Fulton, 2014, *Global Career Management Best Practices Research Report*)

Top performing organizations in terms of career management tended to do so across the board, reporting better overall HR and business performance.

There is clearly an enormously strong business case for supporting your leaders to be able to deliver better quality development discussions that either supplement or replace the traditional performance conversation. There is obvious positive business impact directly linked to organizational financial performance when you enable leaders to get insight into the motivators and engagers of each employee, and empower your leaders to customize a retention and engagement proposition for each employee and unlock the potential within your business.

Furthermore, there is also a clear business case for investing in a "best-practice career management model" across the business. The next part of this book will showcase how to create customized retention and engagement propositions for each employee, while the final part will share the "best practice" model of career engagement which is being utilized by thought-leading HR practitioners and business leaders across the globe.

NOTES

1   This chapter draws on the research in Crawley, M. and Fulton, A. *Global Career Management Best Practices Research Report*. In Press (2014).
2   Ibid.
3   For scientific meta-analyses of leader effectiveness see Judge and Piccolo (2004); Avolio, Walumba and Weber (2009).
4   For example, Gerstner and Day (1997), and Sin, Nahrgang and Morgeson (2009).
5   See Sonnentag et al. (2012); Karatepe et al. (2014).
6   For biophysiological studies linking evaluative threat to stress response see Thayer et al. (2009).
7   Material in this and subsequent sections of the chapter is based on Crawley, M. and Fulton, A.. *Global Career Management Best Practices Research*. In Press (2014).
8   Crawley, M. and Fulton, A. (2014). *Global Career Management Best Practices Research Report*. In Press.
9   Ibid.

PART B
Individual Tactics for Career Engagement

5 Shaping Career Value Propositions

**And the concept of
Career Capital**

Building career capital in your employees allows you to get "hot" and "sticky" with them.

CREATING "HOT" AND "STICKY" EMPLOYEES

Well, yes, of course we know that you are not allowed to get "hot and sticky with your employees" in the twenty-first century — HR or legal would be onto you in a flash, quicker than you can say the words "sexual harassment."

However, given that "hot" employees are those that are engaged and motivated, and truly bring their passions to work, we would argue that they are highly desirable. You know them when you see them — they have a spark in their eyes, a fire in their belly and they just can't wait to get on with the tasks in front of them. We've seen it in people collecting rubbish from the streets in the way they engage with those around them; we've seen it in customs officials, the ones with a bit of banter and an interest in every person they greet, and we've seen it in a succession of baristas who have made our coffee memorable through the service they offer. It's these ones with the spark that we remember and while they do not necessarily have to be in your Talent, High Potential or Accelerate program, they are the people you want in your business because they are the ones that inevitably end up getting noticed. They are the truly engaged employees with a special personal spark that lights up the work they do and those around you.

But while a "hot" attitude is what we want from our employees we also need them to be "sticky;" in other words retained, engaged and committed to you. We already know from previous chapters that because of the talent wars happening now and through social media (think LinkedIn, Facebook and Twitter) your "hot" employees are more visible than ever to the rest of the world, especially your competition.

Creating "sticky-ness" in your employees requires you to understand exactly what these employees really want:

- What lights their fire?

- Which talents do they want to use and develop?

- What are their personal underlying motivators and drivers?

Are they loving their work?
Customizing a career proposition for these employees through tailoring a career path and opportunities around their talents, values and motivators is the answer to retention. And it's easier to put in place than you might think once you have insight to these key factors. Often these employees are only looking for minor tweaks to their roles, or small opportunities to contribute more value, or use more of their "hidden" talents. Micro shaping their roles does not need to cost a lot of money or be difficult for management to put in place, but it can have a macro impact on the engagement and satisfaction of that employee, which will ultimately deliver a direct result on the sticky-ness of that employee.

It comes down to the simple fact that if your "hot" employees are loving their work and growing their career with you, they will be less tempted to look elsewhere. Daniel Pink has shown us that most people are not motivated by money.[1] Creating "hot", engaged and "sticky" employees is easier than you think.

CAREER VALUE PROPOSITIONS

Customizing career propositions is the answer to driving up your retention statistics and driving down your turnover and attrition statistics. If each employee knows how "growing their career with you" is going to make a positive difference to their enjoyment of work right now and also contribute to their future, you are more likely to retain them. A customized career proposition is an extension of your employee value proposition (EVP) and needs careful consideration as part of any communication, written or spoken, relating to your EVP.

> **Customizing career propositions is the answer to driving up your retention statistics and driving down your turnover and attrition statistics.**

Given the current widespread interest in retention practices and the ongoing talent wars, it is essential to build compelling retention plans in order to retain valued contributors and circumvent serious attrition issues in the immediate future. The key to thriving in the current talent climate is the ability to articulate a strong career value proposition, allowing you to distinguish yourself from competitors and to promote your business as an employer of choice.

The key to enhancing the power of your employer brand rests upon the formulation of an attractive employee value proposition, which communicates the offerings that you as an organization will provide each employee in return for the talents and experiences an employee brings to the organization.[2] The primary goal of the EVP proposition is to clarify the relative expectations of employee contributions and the benefits they can expect in return in a formalized manner, strengthening the internal and external reputation of your organization as an employer of choice. The concept of the EVP as an effective way to increase retention stems from research demonstrating the relevance of marketing principles to HR and vice versa.

Both the EVP and the related concept of career value proposition (CVP) are extensions of the "psychological contract," which has been firmly established as a powerful determinant of key employment outcomes.[3] The psychological contract refers to judgments regarding mutual "give and take" that employees make when weighing the value of their current employment situation and determining how much effort and energy to invest in their roles. However, these judgments are not static and employers should avoid making the assumption that a contract is something that is signed only once upon recruitment. Nor is engagement something that happens once a year during a performance review.

 Engagement is the sum of small everyday actions as employees are constantly re-evaluating their attitudes towards their work and tweaking their commitment levels accordingly as they "sign up" for work each morning.[4]

Recent research into the underlying psychology of employee engagement shows that meaningful work corresponds to personal talents, supportive working conditions, and meaningful opportunities for career development, which in turn impact engagement, organizational commitment, as well as long-term career success.[5] Even small changes to bring work into closer alignment with your employees' personal preferences signal that you are making a commitment to them. This in turn increases the reciprocal commitment from the side of employees, who respond by increasing discretional effort and engagement, and improving performance.[6] In short, they start to go that extra mile and place more value on their contract with your organization. In marketing terms, these practices may be said to increase your employer brand, your contractual bargaining power, and consequently, your ability to attract, engage and therefore retain talent on a daily basis.

CAREER CAPITAL: WHAT IS IT AND HOW CAN IT HELP YOU?

As well as boosting your attractiveness as an employer of choice, well-formulated EVPs also work to drive up your retention statistics and reduce your turnover and attrition statistics on a more subtle level by allowing your employees to build "career capital." Career capital is the asset base that you build when you add personal skills and competencies to your unique talent-bank.[7] Just as over a lifetime we can accumulate assets and wealth if we invest wisely, so it is for our careers. When we add to our skills, experience and competencies, we are increasing our personal career capital. We are more employable, we have added protection or insurance against redundancy or redeployment, and our confidence and contributions to our organizations grow.

Career capital today is all about improving your personal marketability. When career capital is built, you are increasing your employees' personal career capital, forming a buffer against redundancy and ensuring a competitive edge within a rapidly evolving labor market. Research shows that employees are increasingly conscious of their career capital, as the mass layoffs and restructuring plans of recent years have irrevocably dented the faith that they once held in their employers, changing employment relations on a fundamental level.[8]

Employees no longer expect to work for one employer in a steady manner for the duration of their working life, and so classic retention strategies based on job security have long since given way to a **new economy of employee benefits based on development and growth opportunities**.[9] As people become more employable, their confidence in their own employability grows, and their commitment to the organization they work for deepens reciprocally in return for such opportunities.

Investing in the career capital of employees does not necessarily involve large and costly changes. In fact, research from our own career agility data suggests that 75% of individuals are willing to invest their own time and resources in development.

According to our own career agility data, 75% of individuals are willing to invest their own time and resources in development.

Small steps, such as redesigning tasks, stretch assignments, and mentoring provide valuable developmental opportunities at little or no additional cost. Activities such as mentoring are particularly useful as they provide benefits for both mentor and mentoree. Mentoring represents a valuable coaching and leadership experience, and is an effective means to engage Baby Boomer generation employees and keep them contributing long past what would have been their original retirement dates.[10] Furthermore, these adjustments produce broader positive spin-offs for resolving additional HR challenges, such as leadership development and succession planning, which are considered to be the most pressing HR issues at this moment.[11]

PERSONAL REFLECTION

What is your career capital balance? Like financial capital, career capital is the sum of your career assets at any given time. The balance can be increased through good investments in your career such as networking, secondments and training. But it can also be depleted through neglect and career-limiting moves, such as remaining focused on the past, negativity, and a reluctance to develop new skills. When individuals continue to grow their career capital balance, they are in a much stronger position to deal with unexpected changes in their employment.

THE UNIQUE SELLING PROPOSITION (USP) AND CAREER CAPITAL

Successful career value propositions allow employees to build career capital in a manner that reflects their own uniquely defined set of skills and experiences. This allows them to strengthen their personal brand by developing their personal marketability through their own unique selling proposition that they offer potential employers. Certain job tasks or functions are fairly standardized, and can be best performed by "clones" with a well-defined skill-set, such as process workers on an assembly line. Increasingly, however, an organization's employees need to develop skills that enhance their own unique brand of personal marketability in order to truly support the agile organization of the future.

It is essential to balance skills training for defined business outcomes against developmental opportunities that allow people to grow their skills in a unique and personally defined way. It is also essential that the employees themselves are involved in this process, which can be achieved by talking to them, and finding out their career ambitions and drivers. Offering developmental opportunities without first consulting with the individuals in question can actually have the reverse effect in that training or stretch assignments, which do not align with personal circumstances and career goals, are easily perceived as a burden. However, involving employees in decisions regarding their own career paths fosters a sense of empowerment, which is profoundly motivating.

 The employee comes to "own" their career by taking responsibility for the architecture of their chosen path and their commitment to the organization grows in consequence.

THE CAREER CONVERSATION: FEEL THE FEAR AND DO IT ANYWAY

Despite the effectiveness of personalized career building opportunities as a means to retain talent, many managers fear that investing in employee development will encourage employees to leave, or increase the likelihood of them being "poached" or lured away by a competitor. However, this fear has been shown to be unfounded; in fact the reverse is true. Failing to engage your employees in meaningful career discussions and offering developmental opportunities is an almost certain way to bring about the very outcomes you seek to avoid. With "lack of significant development and career advancement" cited as primary causes for voluntary turnover,[12] business leaders and research statistics agree that if you don't have those conversations, and if you don't find out what skills and talents your employees most want to use at work, they are far more likely to leave.[13] Such practice is akin to keeping your head in the sand, and failing to keep pace with talent management practices is a form of denial.

Customizing career value propositions involves identifying the critical career "engagers" or satisfaction factors that are going to impact an individual's "intent to stay." (See the panel "How to Customize Career Propositions" on page 82.)

HOW TO CUSTOMIZE CAREER PROPOSITIONS

Customizing career propositions can be easy.

- The first step involves finding out what the engagers and motivators are for each person. In Chapter 6 we look in more detail at how to identify the career "sweet spot" for your employees, but in the meantime it's all about asking simple questions such as: What excites you most about your work? What are you doing when you are most "into" your work and lose track of time? Questions like this will enable your leaders and managers to gain quick insight into the "sweet spots" for each employee.

- The next step is to look for simple ways to create an opportunity for an employee to get more of that activity, the ones that inspire them, in their ongoing work.

- Thirdly, find opportunities for action to be taken and commit to it. It is often about creating small opportunities for your employee to use a talent or contribute more for them to feel more engaged.

- Finally, make sure you check in regularly about how your employees are tracking in developing their skills and talents. In this way, employees are aware that you are delivering on promise and they are getting a unique opportunity to add to their skill base and future marketability.

HOW BUILDING INDIVIDUAL CAREER CAPITAL IMPACTS YOUR RETENTION OUTCOMES

Why should you invest in building the careers of your employees? Won't they just leave after all that effort? This is a common cry from managers fearful of having career conversations with their employees. However, the truth is if you don't have those conversations, if you don't find out what skills and talents your employees most want to use at work, of course they are far more likely to leave you.

It does not have to be expensive or time-consuming. Our own Career Agility Trends Research showed that over 75% of people were willing to use their own time to invest in their learning.[14] And smart organizations are providing technology enablers for their employees to continue learning and growing.

Some of the best learning experiences for people happen on the job. Opportunities for mentoring (even informal mentoring programs) can provide some of the most valuable learning experiences for people. It is an inexpensive way for career growth for both individual employees and their mentors. As discussed earlier, it has been found that mentors can grow their own personal skills by becoming involved, which can often be a skill that more experienced employees are keen to develop.

To summarize, career propositions will impact engagement outcomes in your organization. If you can enable each and every manager to get insight into the engagers and motivators of every employee this can be the fastest and simplest way to build engagement across the entire organization. Clearly, there will be differences, and often the difference in satisfaction and engagement can be manipulated in micro ways to gain significant outcomes. If every employee can see how they are growing their career capital and personal marketability, and they have an exciting personalized career proposition with your organization, you are well on the way to building your career EVP, your business reputation as an employer of choice and retaining your talent.

Organizations in which people are fully leveraging the talent, skills and passion of their people will have a more engaged and productive workforce and a stronger EVP.

Investing in the career capital of your people brings significant positive outcomes to your organization in that you will have employees with increased confidence and the ability to add more value to their work. Your organization will develop a reputation and brand as an employer of choice, and it will become known as the kind of place where people aspire to work because they will gain great skills and experience. In essence, your business employment brand and EVP are inextricably related to your ability to deliver increased career capital to your employees.

TIPS FOR MANAGERS

- Watch out for those occasions when your employees seem to be most engaged and absorbed in their work; they are probably playing to their natural talents.

- Take the time to ask employees to tell you which aspects of their work they love the most. Ask them: what kind of tasks and activities would you like to do more of if given the chance?

- The converse also applies, so be sure to ask them about the aspects of their work they find most challenging or arduous. Ask: How can I help to manage this aspect of your work?

- Ask them to tell you whose work they admire across the business. Ask: How can I give you an opportunity to learn from those people?

NOTES

1 Pink, D.H. (2011). *Drive: The Surprising Truth About What Motivates Us*. Penguin, New York, NY.

2 Minchington, B. (2010). *Employer Brand Leadership: A Global Perspective*. Collective Learning Australia, Torrensville, South Australia.

3 Inkson, K. and King, Z. (2011). Contested terrain in careers: A psychological contract model. *Human Relations*, 64(1), 37–57.

4 For a summary and empirical case study linking work conditions to commitment levels see Maguire, H. (2002). Psychological contracts: Are they still relevant? *Career Development International*, 7(3), 167–80.

5 For empirical studies see: Botha, Bussin and De Swardt (2011); Vijayakumar and Parvin (2010); De Vos, De Hauw and Van der Heijden (2011); Tims, Bakker and Derks (2012; 2013).

6 Maguire, H. (2002). Psychological contracts: Are they still relevant? *Career Development International*, 7(3), 167–80; Inkson, K. and King, Z. (2011). Contested terrain in careers: A psychological contract model. *Human Relations*, 64(1), 37–57; Ng, T.W. and Feldman, D.C. (2012). Breaches of past promises, current job alternatives, and promises of future idiosyncratic deals: Three-way interaction effects on organizational commitment. *Human Relations*, 65(11), 1463–86; Bakker, A.B., Demerouti, E. and Sanz-Vergel, A.I. (2014). Burnout and work engagement: The JD-R approach. *Annual Review of Organizational Psychology and Organizational Behavior*, 1, 389–411.

7 Inkson, K. and Arthur, M.B. (2001). How to be a successful career capitalist. *Organizational Dynamics*, 30(1), 48–61.

8 See Benko, C. and Weisberg, A. (2007). *Mass Career Customization: Aligning the Workplace with Today's Nontraditional Workforce*. Harvard Business Review Press, Boston, Massachusetts; Benko, C. and Anderson, M. (2010). *The Corporate Lattice: Achieving High Performance in the Changing World of Work*. Harvard Business Review Press, Boston, Massachusetts.

9 Maguire, H. (2002). Psychological contracts: Are they still relevant? *Career Development International,* 7(3), 167–80, and Benko, C. and Anderson, M. (2010), op. cit.

10 See Warr, P. (2001). Age and work behavior: Physical attributes, cognitive abilities, knowledge, personality traits, and motives. *International Review of Industrial and Organizational Psychology*, 16, 1–36.

11 Benko, C., Erickson, R., Hagel, J. and Wong, J. (2014). *Beyond Retention: Build Passion and Purpose*. Deloitte University Press. Retrieved from: http://dupress.com/ articles/ hc-trends-2014-beyond-retention/.

12 *Talentkeepers Global Talent and Retention Report 2013*. Retrieved from: www. talentkeepers.com/download/2013-TalentKeepers-Employee-Engagement-Retention-Trends-Report-Final.pdf.

13 Benson, G.S. (2006). Employee development, commitment and intention to turnover: A test of "employability" policies in action. *Human Resource Management Journal*, 16(2), 173–92; Allen, D.G., Shore, L.M. and Griffeth, R.W. (2003). The role of perceived organizational support and supportive human resource practices in the turnover process. *Journal of Management*, 29(1), 99–118; and Chen, T.Y., Chang, P.L. and Yeh, C.W. (2004). A study of career needs, career development programs, job satisfaction and the turnover intentions of R&D personnel. *Career Development International*, 9(4), 424–37.

14 Fuel50 (2013). *Career Agility Trends Research*. Retrieved from: www.fuel50.com/pdf/ career-agility-engagement-fuel50-white-paper.pdf

6 | Work Shaping

Micro tweaks for Macro impact on engagement

Even small changes towards aligning working conditions with employee preferences result in increased engagement levels.

WORK SHAPING FOR SATISFACTION AND ENGAGEMENT

It is possible to improve the "motivational potential" of every role and for every employee in your organization by utilizing the scientifically validated approach of "work shaping" as we describe it or "job sculpting" as it is known in the academic literature.[1] Joint ownership for work shaping works best when a manager facilitates and enables work shaping to happen and an employee is given the resources and opportunity to make some "shaping" changes to their role.

At the organizational level, work-shaping practices have been shown to make substantial differences in engagement and satisfaction indices, resulting in decreased attrition and, ultimately, an improved bottom line.[2] Examples of these practices include enabling the formulation of a customized career proposition for every employee by empowering managers and employees to have the autonomy for some levels of job shaping and integrating strategic career discussions as a core HR practice at all levels of the organization.

Rather than offering a prescribed one-size-fits-all solution, talent management policies provide a strategy that can be tailored to fit the needs of the individual and the organization in question. Job redesign interventions that bolster employee engagement by tailoring the specific work environment and job redesign have received considerable empirical support as a means to engage and retain employees.[3]

Improving compatibility and alignment

Work shaping is designed to improve the compatibility and alignment between an employee and their work. Compatibility is not a simple construct, and in reality most people find themselves positioned somewhere along a compatibility continuum. An individual can be compatible with some aspects of a job, while finding other aspects grating. Equally, they may be an excellent fit for their current role in terms of talents and skills, yet fail to relate to the people within the organization itself or the broader organizational mission.

According to our thinking here at Fuel50, compatibility grows progressively as the employee and the employer connect across multiple levels of a needs hierarchy.

 The greater the alignment across all levels of this compatibility pyramid, the greater commitment to the job the employee will experience.

This enhanced commitment leads to higher engagement, increased discretionary effort and optimum performance.

These levels can be conceived of as a pyramid akin to that proposed by Maslow with his hierarchy of motivational needs.[4] The lower level material needs associated with physical and transactional role requirements sit below the more aspirational needs relating to contribution, self-actualization and deeper meaning. In some circumstances, as we shall see, high levels of compatibility between higher aspirational needs relating to identity and values, which sit at the top of the pyramid, can override lower level material needs such as salary.

We like to think of work shaping from both a strategic and a tactical perspective. It can range from transformative, strategic career reviews (career shaping at a macro level) through to the tactical work shaping that can occur through making micro tweaks to job roles that can deliver a significant effect on job engagement (see Fig. 6.1).

The work-shaping pyramid

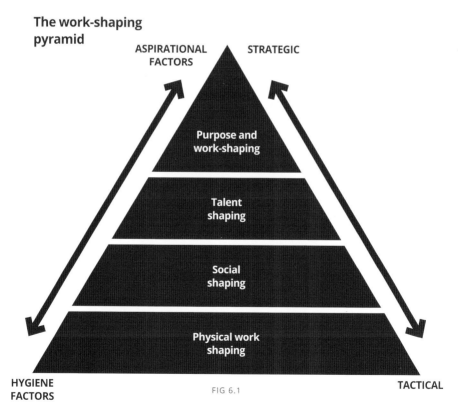

ASPIRATIONAL FACTORS   STRATEGIC

Purpose and work-shaping

Talent shaping

Social shaping

Physical work shaping

HYGIENE FACTORS

FIG 6.1

TACTICAL

We believe that Maslow's valuable work on human motivation can be adapted as a useful model for both employees and business leaders to utilize in order to make effective (and often inexpensive and subtle) changes to work experience that lead to increased engagement and productivity. Although Maslow's theory has been critiqued and developed over the years, it is a widely understood model that can be applied to work shaping in a simple and practical way by both employees and managers.

The work-shaping pyramid helps explain how career and work shaping can be applied in practice. We start with the basic or physical work-shaping needs at the base of the pyramid, moving up to higher order or aspirational factors. At the base of the pyramid is where tactical or micro work-shaping factors can be adapted through to the strategic factors at the top of the hierarchy.

LEVEL 1: PHYSICAL WORK SHAPING

Maslow's hierarchy of needs starts with physiological (food, water, sleep) and safety needs (security of health, employment, family etc.). For our model, we focus first on physical work factors for work-shaping purposes. These can include location, hours, employment contracts (particularly relating to job security), work flexibility, and specific work tasks that are agreed and which are non-negotiable in the role.

Generally, adjustments to these foundational work aspects are organizationally controlled and managed, and any changes to work experiences at this level will need to be negotiated with an employee's immediate manager if not HR.

The 2013 global Career Agility Trends survey, completed by over 1100 respondents, tracked responses to key career trends, including work–life balance preferences and attitudes to flexible work practices, and it highlighted some key differences in the career "wants" of men and women.

Work–life balance examples

Some 61% of respondents wanted to work four days or fewer and 36% of respondents would prefer to work four days per week, even if this meant some salary sacrifice. Perhaps organizations that are struggling with cash flow can bring back some of the work practices of nine-day fortnights or four-day weeks that flourished during the Global Financial Crisis.

Surprisingly, there were also 6% of respondents who were keen to work longer days, such as 10 or 12-hour shifts.

> *Bruce, a 42-year-old electrician currently working on the Gold Coast in Australia, prefers to work 12-hour shifts because of the flexibility that it gives him. "I do seven big days then get four straight days off, which allows me to go surfing, diving or camping if I want to. I will also work big hours for a contract for say nine months and then have three months off to go skiing in the US or Canada, or diving in the Maldives."*

While this works well for some, others struggle or have mixed feelings with extended hours.

> *As Nicola, a nurse at a large hospital, describes, "While I love the days off that come with working three 12-hour shifts a week, I find I am so exhausted after three of them that it takes me at least a day to recover. I also find that I dread the thought of going to work when I am working a 12-hour day shift, purely due to the fact that it is such a long day and come 5pm it really does feel like home time!"*

These two examples show the importance of understanding individual needs and drivers, as no two people will be identical in career and lifestyle wants. Giving employees the opportunity to make these "tactical" adjustments to their work experiences can positively impact their sense of personal work satisfaction and work–life fit. Our global Career Agility Trends Research also showed that most people want around four hours per month in terms of flexibility. It is often literally about having the opportunity to fit in that dentist appointment or treat yourself to a game of golf or hair appointment.

Younger people also had significantly higher leadership aspirations and had aspirations of leading a team or being part of senior management teams in the future.

> *Jonny, a young Gen Y financial services manager, typifies this view, commenting, "A leadership role is certainly the goal. I believe the ability to manage not just the workload, but also people, is a key aspect in developing my career and will no doubt be a large part of success in future years."*

However, a surprising 70% of those aged over 50 were either not interested in leading a team at all or wanted to lead only a small team of people. This fits with the finding that Baby Boomers were more likely to want to reduce the pace of their work. We found that younger people wanted significantly more career growth and to be fast-tracked in their careers, while the older workers in the survey wanted to reduce their workloads and work responsibilities. Employers may need to consider fast-tracking the careers of younger people to ensure they have a leadership pipeline in the future.

These examples show how important tactical and environmental work shaping can be to the career engagement of your individual employees. A regular conversation with your employees on their basic work needs should be conducted on an annual basis as a bare minimum, to contribute to optimum career engagement. Diagnostics such as Fuel50 and the Deloitte MCC profile that the employees use to reflect on and articulate their career wants and needs can contribute significantly to the effectiveness of the conversation.

GAINING LEVERAGE OVER A JOB

Ricardo Semler, the CEO and majority owner of Semco SA, a Brazilian company best known for its radical form of industrial democracy and corporate re-engineering, allowed its workers to set their own production quotas and found that employees would voluntarily work overtime to meet them. This is not surprising to us, as our Career Engagement Research showed that 75% of people wanted to contribute more to their organizations. Semler encapsulates the sentiment in his autobiography, Maverick![5] when he says: "A great deal of employee satisfaction occurs when individuals have some leverage over the logistics of their job."

LEVEL 2: SOCIAL WORK SHAPING

Social factors

The second level we refer to from Maslow's hierarchy of needs is social factors. In Maslow's language this is described as a need for love and a sense of belonging. In a work context we see this playing out as a need for social contact and the sense of belonging relates to people's need for teamwork. Our research shows teamwork is reported as a career value of primary or secondary importance for a large proportion of employees.

When it comes to work shaping, focusing on our social needs can also be an important aspect. In the academic literature it is described as relationship shaping, where an individual has an opportunity to add, strengthen or even reduce work relationships based on their individual needs and career aspirations.[6] So, if an employee wants to find a mentor to assist with a particular skill development this would be a classic example of shaping work experiences from a relationship perspective.

Understanding the importance of relationship aspects is a fundamental part of building a strong personal career plan.

We may deliver value to others in our work network, which can open doors for future opportunities. Or perhaps we leverage relationships for the learning opportunities that ensue. Both are examples of extending a social network and shaping relationships, which can be very low cost ways of increasing work satisfaction and adding to the future career capital and marketability of your employees. It is a simple and often quick win for both parties.

Esteem needs

Maslow's theory also talked of esteem needs as being important. For the purposes of our model, we see these esteem needs being met by the social or relational aspects of work. Personal esteem can be gained by getting feedback from others, whether customers, colleagues or managers. Building your reputation and extending your sphere of influence are important career growth factors. Looking at how your work can be shaped to address these factors can be a useful dialogue starter for employees and their managers.

Again Fuel50 (along with many other psychometric assessments) can identify how much appreciation an employee needs for their personal satisfaction. If this is identified it becomes a very simple motivation enhancement tactic that a manager can take into their ongoing leadership and management of that employee. This is so easy to facilitate when a leader understands it is a driver for an employee. It can cost you nothing to deliver an immediate and ongoing impact on career satisfaction and work engagement.

SHAPING FOR SELF-ACTUALIZATION: TALENT-ACTUALIZING AND PURPOSE ALIGNMENT

The final level in Maslow's hierarchy of needs is self-actualizing: "What a man can be, he must be."[7] This quotation forms the basis of the perceived need for self-actualization. This level of need refers to what a person's full potential is and the realization of that potential. Maslow describes this level as the desire to accomplish everything that one can, to become the most that one can be.[8] He believed that to understand this level of need, the person must not only achieve the previous needs, but master them.[9]

For our proposed model for career and work shaping we believe that Maslow's self-actualization need can be split into two separate factors for work-shaping purposes that require individual attention.

- Firstly, talent actualization involves using your innate talents that need to be expressed: according to Maslow if we have certain "gifts" we need to express and grow these capabilities. Work shaping which focuses on talent actualization can have a significant impact on career satisfaction and work engagement. This is Level 3 in our model.

- The second factor from our experience and perspective is around purpose and meaning (Level 4 in our work-shaping model). We believe that the majority of people have an innate drive for purpose which can be articulated and extended through work. We will look at each of these factors separately.

LEVEL 3: TALENT SHAPING

The fit between talents and abilities

The third level of compatibility relates to the fit between the talents and abilities of the individual employee and those required for high performance in the role. It is critical to ensure that the largest portion of any job is a good or at least reasonable reflection of the employee's true strengths. Research published by the Gallup Institute (2013) confirms that Generation X, Millennials, and Baby Boomers are at their most engaged when they have the opportunity to "do what they do best" every day.[10]

If we persist in a role that is a poor fit to our true abilities, we may be able to produce a high or acceptable level of performance, but this is not likely to be sustainable. This is because we will need to exert more effort to achieve these results compared to the effort exerted by a person who is naturally "talented" at these tasks. Although there may be no apparent difference in performance between these two individuals, the less "talented" employee will need to exert greater effort to maintain a given level of performance and thus it will be achieved at greater personal cost.

Ultimately, maintaining high-level performance at tasks for which we have scant affinity leaves us vulnerable to burnout and stress-related fatigue. On the other hand, being *good* at something is naturally motivating, and it is easy to keep doing tasks we are good at because we get a sense of achievement with relatively little exerted effort.

Being good at something is naturally motivating, and it is easy to keep doing tasks we are good at because we get a sense of achievement with relatively little exerted effort.

Balancing what we are good at with what we enjoy

However, just because an employee is *good at* a given task does not mean that they:

- Enjoy the task

- Want to perform that task

- Find that task fulfilling

In reality, the laws of human nature tend to ensure a reasonable degree of congruence between what we are good at and what we enjoy, and as a result the distinction becomes rather blurred. At times, it can be very difficult to distinguish between the two. The praise and sense of contribution we receive when we excel create a positive emotion that is easy to confuse with *liking* that activity. When we are good at something we tend to get praised for our performance, and we also receive more opportunities to do this activity. As a result, we keep getting better at what we are already good at as we accrue experience. While this can be seen as nature's way of guiding us towards livelihoods that provide greater rewards in return for the effort we expend, it is not sufficient to ensure continued engagement. Sustained engagement and wellbeing at work requires that we also feel an emotional connection to the work, identify with the broader sense of mission that we accomplish, and are able to move towards our truest selves.

Talent realization

In Maslow's model, realizing one's talent potential is a higher order need, and we believe that this is a driver that is in play for all employees. Everyone wants a sense that their work is using their unique skills and capabilities, and optimally that there is an opportunity to extend those capabilities and reach their full potential. As discussed in our next chapter, we understand that identifying motivated talents and creating plans to develop them is critical to effective career development, and from the organizational perspective leveraging more of the talents that exist within your organization makes great business sense.

Everyone wants a sense that their work is using their unique skills and capabilities.

According to Clifton and Harter, work shaping in ways that facilitates employees leveraging more of their skills and talents at work (whether it is problem solving, or attention to detail) can contribute to meaningfulness of work by "helping employees to leverage what they are naturally capable of doing well."[11]

LEVEL 4: PURPOSE AND WORK SHAPING

In order to achieve sustainable performance it is not sufficient to concentrate exclusively on what we do well. We also need to find meaning in what we are doing, and to integrate it with our personal identity and passions.

 Research shows that employees have a fundamental desire to find meaning in their work.[12]

Furthermore, in contemporary Western society we are increasingly defined by the work we carry out, which forms the basis for both how others perceive us and how we perceive ourselves. Our work defines what we are able to contribute to society, and as such, it is intrinsically connected to our sense of personal and social identity, as well as our sense of self-worth.[13]

TALENT ACTUALIZATION AND TASKS

Talent actualization through work shaping will focus on three things: adding tasks, emphasizing tasks and/or redesigning tasks (as per Berg, Dutton and Wrzesniewski's model).[14] We also add another item to the model: task minimization.

- **Adding tasks** can be achieved easily in most organizations. The best example is where an individual employee is given a project that leverages their natural talents, such as the administrative person who is given the tasks of researching and implementing a new system or process, or the contact center team member who is given the task of buddying and mentoring a new employee as "coaching and training" is one of their motivated talent areas.

- **Emphasizing tasks** is where employees are given an opportunity to focus more on certain tasks that play to their talents. This is again often a given, as in reality if you put any two people into the same role they will inevitably end up doing things slightly differently and focusing on different aspects of the jobs which utilizes their talents. For example, we can have two managers with an identical job title but, in terms of focus, one brings real analytical strengths and is always presenting great spreadsheets, while a second manager may have strong innate talents around presentation skills and is known for her motivational and influential presentations and speeches. In more transactional roles we can still see this playing out, even on a production line, where we have one person showing a talent for quality attention and another line-worker a talent for motivating teamwork.

- **Redesigning tasks** so that while the same output is achieved, the employee is given more scope in how a task is delivered and to add meaningfulness. Task redesign could include the auditor who gravitates towards taking the lead in client relationship management or the sales team member who takes ownership for collating team metrics.

- **Task minimization** is where non-preferred tasks are minimized, delegated or given lower priority in line with other talents that an individual may offer. An example may be the marketing coordinator who struggles with proofreading tasks, in which another colleague may excel. In these instances some task shaping can be a win–win for both employees if a manager can see the motivated talents and least preferred skills of all team members. In some jobs there are certain "non-negotiables" and tasks which we may all prefer not to do; however, playing to a person's talents and minimizing the frustrations with certain tasks can positively impact satisfaction.

Finding meaning and purpose

Author Viktor Frankl, psychiatrist and Holocaust survivor, provides us with a penetrating observation from his time imprisoned on the connection between our work, actions and intrinsic sense of self and personal identity.[15] Frankl observed that the ability to survive within the extreme conditions of a concentration camp was surprisingly not dependent on physical strength and brute force. Rather, what appeared to make all the difference was the intellectual life of the inmate, in particular the ability to maintain their sense of values and find meaning during the horrific experience of incarceration.

This led Frankl to observe in his classic book *Man's Search For Meaning* that "if a man has a why he can live through any how."

While the horrors of labor camps are a far cry from the boardrooms of today, this does not diminish the importance of personal values, passion and purpose for propelling us out of bed in the morning. A sense of meaning and purpose is what inspires us to persist and overcome the various challenges that are part of any professional undertaking, especially when we are being challenged and growing in our role. A recent meta-analysis published by the Gallup Institute (2014) found that increased job engagement has a greater effect on employee wellbeing than any number of extravagant perks, ranging from flexible working conditions and free lunches to massages. This examination of the work attitudes of thousands of employees concluded that "an intrinsic connection to one's work and one's company is what truly drives performance, inspires discretionary effort, and improves wellbeing."[16]

If a man has a why he can live through any how.

— VIKTOR FRANKL

Values and resilience

The meaning that employees attribute to their work has a profound influence on all aspects of the work experience that goes beyond the desire to achieve. Our values form a buffer against negative job-related stress by allowing us to reframe more tedious and onerous tasks in a positive light. When we are able to understand how our values relate to both the task that we perform and the broader organizational mission, we become more resilient in the face of setbacks, and tasks which would otherwise be draining become a source of emotional fulfillment.[17]

It is not doing the thing we like to do, but liking the thing we have to do, that makes life blessed.

— JOHANN WOLFGANG VON GOETHE

Tom Fernandes, CEO of Luck Corporation, noted during an inspirational presentation at a recent international HR conference that "values-driven organizations are not 'fluffy', they are fierce competitors!",[18] and organizational psychology has proved him right. Meaning has been shown to influence work motivation,[19] work behavior,[20] engagement, job satisfaction, empowerment, stress, organizational performance, as well as personal fulfillment. A consideration of personal values and how these relate to work allows us to move beyond a superficial conception of work in which the individual trades a service for monetary remuneration to a deeper, more holistic approach that taps into underlying notions of purpose and significance.

PURPOSE ALIGNMENT

At the top of the work-shaping model are purpose and meaning as, without question, these will significantly impact career engagement, and we see purpose alignment at work as greatly important. In the context of work shaping, however, we can see this playing out in a few ways.

The research literature talks of cognitive shaping or reframing and this is an important factor in people's career experience.[21] We have seen many a production line worker or contact center agent who has an incredibly strong sense of purpose at work, and this can often be about fundamental personal drivers such as putting dependent children through school, earning sufficient money to pay for relatives "back home" or being able to contribute to their church's mission. This is where purpose alignment can be a very real driver for performance at work.

On another level we see purpose alignment becoming of significant importance to the individual who will want to align at some level with the purpose of their organization, whether it is about environmentally friendly solutions, or "creating better workplaces" as in our own business. Often a significant factor in motivating performance and enhancing engagement is when individuals understand their core business purpose and where their personal alignment point lies.

We also see purpose alignment as relating to the work-shaping factor that is referenced in the emerging literature — this is the concept of work shaping through cognitive reframing.[22] This is a powerful tool for creating meaningfulness at work and is at play when we have the street sweeper who reframes his mundane job as "making a better place for those around me" or for the hospital orderly who reframes his work as "being part of creating a health-improving environment for others."

 Work shaping is a dynamic and ongoing process that empowers employees to realize their innate potential, while also ensuring that organizational needs are met in an efficient and cost-effective manner.

Just as the skilled sculptor knows that the success of their work depends on recognizing and enhancing the innate qualities of the materials at hand, the skilled leader seeks to understand individual employee preferences, and shapes work experiences accordingly. This process, based on mutual respect and ongoing communication, ensures an engaged and motivated workforce, while simultaneously strengthening the employer's "brand" and increasing their ability to attract and retain talent in an increasingly competitive job market.

Providing a deeper connection
Based on the knowledge that job security and benefit packages are ineffective strategies for motivating and retaining talent, work shaping leverages the intrinsic sense of mastery and satisfaction that results from using innate talents and meaningful work to engage employees.[23]

As employees begin to own their careers and architect their work experiences, they are able to connect to their work at a deeper level, resulting in increased commitment, discretionary effort, and that contagious sense of passion that inspires customers and key stakeholders alike.

As part of an organization's talent philosophy, work shaping is an effective means to ensure the talent pool remains calibrated to organizational needs, as developmental opportunities and continued employment depend on high-level performance outcomes.

Facilitating work shaping

Although it is necessary for the employer to provide the overarching mandate that supports work shaping, the responsibility for successful work shaping must be a joint venture between the organization and the employee. The organization's responsibility is to provide the mandate, the tools or enablers, the talent framework and the sponsorship of work shaping as an effective means of delivering positive business outcomes. The organization must ensure that managers have the mandate and skills necessary to support an employee's work-shaping desires.

We have to accept that many job requirements will be "givens" in any role and non-negotiable, but within most roles today there will be "alterable" aspects that can be shaped to fit with the individual preferences and therefore increase what is termed "person–job fit" in the academic literature.[24]

Energizing activities

The organization's responsibility is to enable, support and facilitate a more "worktopian" environment for each and every employee by supporting work shaping. However, your employees ultimately "own" their personal work experience and must engage in honest reflection in order to design their work, goals and their own work–life fit.

Motivational potential is enhanced for every employee as they learn to recognize which aspects of a job are energizing, as opposed to draining. Energizing activities, which are natural motivators in their own right, may then be enhanced through appropriate stretch activities to further increase engagement levels in what becomes a positive gain cycle.[25] In a similar manner, draining activities, which do not play to employees' strengths, may be eliminated, assigned to other employees who may enjoy them more, or be redesigned.

Where this is not possible due to organizational constraints, cognitive reframing techniques may be used to find deeper meaning within less palatable tasks, and strategies may be identified to bolster performance. These cognitive reframing examples show us how powerful it can be when people can connect in a meaningful way to the purpose of their work or the organization they work with. Starbucks is an example of a business that is making this purpose alignment evident to every customer with their "community" campaign in which every store is part of a community and has a responsibility to be a "good neighbor."

STARBUCKS' PURPOSE ALIGNMENT

"We have always believed Starbucks can — and should — have a positive impact on the communities we serve. One person, one cup and one neighborhood at a time.

"As we have grown to now more than 20,000 stores in over 60 countries, so too has our commitment to use our scale for good.

"So it is our vision that together we will elevate our partners, customers, suppliers and neighbors to create positive change. To be innovators, leaders and contributors to an inclusive society and a healthy environment so that Starbucks and everyone we touch can endure and thrive."

It is important to note that work shaping does not require drastic changes based on abstract dreams of desired futures. Rather than focusing on strategic or long-term career moves, work shaping is an immediate tactical process rooted firmly in the here and now. This is where the gold seam of motivational enhancement resides.

Small wins — big gains

Small changes in the individual work experiences that are either owned and initiated by the employee or, even better, are collaboratively agreed with the manager can have immediate impacts on personal motivation and career satisfaction. These are analogous to the tacking changes made in sailing. A boat may be heading directly north but needs to make small tacks constantly to get to the long-term goal. This is true both for the individual's career management and the organization. Business strategic planning cycles have been accelerated and what once were five-year strategic goals are increasingly now 90-day sprints to execute on both tactical and strategic goals. The flow-on effect of this business phenomenon is the increased demand for agility from employees, but equally it is creating an opportunity for employees to constantly re-evaluate what and how they can contribute and leverage their talents to assist with the execution of business goals. The increased shift to agile work teams is also creating opportunity for employees to extend their contributions while simultaneously extending and adding to their talents "asset base" or skills "talent bank."

Agile work shaping is based on the premise that optimal outcomes may be achieved only through win–win situations for both parties, as well as research demonstrating that even small changes towards bringing working conditions into closer alignment with employee preferences result in increased engagement levels and reduced turnover.[26] This, in turn, translates into substantial improvements in bottom-line financial outcomes.[27]

NOTES

1 For example, Breevaart, K., Bakker, A.B. and Demerouti, E. (2014). Daily self-management and employee work engagement. *Journal of Vocational Behavior*, 84(1), 31–38; Berg, J.M., Dutton, J.E. and Wrzesniewski, A. (2008). What is job crafting and why does it matter? Retrieved from: http://positiveorgs.bus.umich.edu/wp-content/uploads/What-is-Job-Crafting-and-Why-Does-it-Matter1.pdf; Bakker, A.B. (2011). An evidence-based model of work engagement. *Current Directions in Psychological Science*, 20(4), 265–69.

2 See Minchington (2010); Benko and Anderson (2010); Vijayakumar and Parvin (2010); Clark (2012); Tims, Bakker and Derks (2013); Bakker, Demerouiti and Sanz-Vergel (2014).

3 For example, Halbesleben, Osburn and Mumford (2006); Le Blanc et al. (2007).

4 Maslow, A. (1954). *Motivation and Personality*. Harper, New York, NY.

5 Semler, R. (1993). *Maverick!: The Success Story Behind the World's Most Unusual Workplace.* Warner Books, New York, NY.

6 For an introduction to the different kinds of job sculpting practices see Berg, J.M., Dutton, J.E. and Wrzesniewski, A. (2008). What is job crafting and why does it matter? Retrieved from: http://positiveorgs.bus.umich.edu/wp-content/uploads/What-is-Job-Crafting-and-Why-Does-it-Matter1.pdf; Tims, M. and Bakker, A.B. (2010). Job crafting: Towards a new model of individual job redesign. *South African Journal of Industrial Psychology*, 36(2), 1–9; or Wrzesniewski, A., LoBuglio, N., Dutton, J.E. and Berg, J.M. (2013). Job crafting and cultivating positive meaning and identity in work. *Advances in Positive Organizational Psychology*, 1, 281–302 for a more detailed discussion.

7 Maslow, A. (1954). *Motivation and Personality*. Harper, New York, NY, p. 91.

8 Ibid., p. 92.

9 The statement is taken from the Wikipedia description of the self-actualization level of Maslow's hierarchy, retrieved from: http://en.wikipedia.org/wiki/Maslow's_hierarchy_of_needs#cite_note-12.

10 The Gallup Institute (2013). *State of the American Workplace: Employee engagement insights for US business leaders*. Retrieved from: www.gallup.com/strategicconsulting/163007/state-american-workplace.aspx.

11 Clifton, D.O. and Harter, J.K. (2003). Investing in strengths. In K.S. Cameron, J.E. Dutton and R.E. Quinn (eds), *Positive Organizational Scholarship: Foundations of a New Discipline*. Berrett-Koehler, San Francisco, pp. 111–21.

12 Rosso, B.D., Dekas, K.H. and Wrzesniewski, A. (2010). On the meaning of work: A theoretical integration and review. *Research in Organizational Behavior*, 30, 91–127.

13 See Gecas, V. (1982). The self-concept. *Annual Review of Psychology*, 8, 1–33; and Wrzesniewski, A. (2003). Finding positive meaning in work. In K.S. Cameron, J.E. Dutton and R.E. Quinn (eds), *Positive Organizational Scholarship: Foundations of a New Discipline*, op. cit., pp. 296–308.

14 Berg, Dutton and Wrzesniewski, A. (2008), op. cit.

15 Frankl, V.E. (1985). *Man's Search for Meaning*. Simon and Schuster, New York, NY.

16 The Gallup Institute (2014). *State of the American Workplace: Employee engagement insights for US business leaders*. Retrieved from: www.gallup.com/strategicconsulting/163007/state-american-workplace.aspx.

17 The theorist generally associated with pioneering the importance of efficacy beliefs as a means to bolster resilience was Bandura (see Bandura A. (*1977*). *Social Learning Theory*. General Learning Press, New York, NY). More recently these ideas have been extended and developed and are currently referred to in the scientific literature as psychological capital; see Luthans, F., Avolio, B.J., Avey, J.B. and Norman, S.M. (2007). Positive psychological capital: Measurement and relationship with performance and satisfaction. *Personnel Psychology*, 60(3), 541–72.

18 Fernandes, M. (2012). *Values Based Leadership*. Retrieved from: http://553.membee.

com/cms/clients/553/files/Leadership_Program_Nov27.pdf.

19 Hackman, J.R. and Oldham, G.R. (1980). *Work Redesign*. Addison-Wesley, Reading, Massachusetts.

20 Berg, J.M., Dutton, J.E. and Wrzesniewski, A. (2008). What is job crafting and why does it matter? Retrieved from: http://positiveorgs.bus.umich.edu/wp-content/uploads/What-is-Job-Crafting-and-Why-Does-it-Matter1.pdf.

21 See Rosso, B.D., Dekas, K H. and Wrzesniewski, A. (2010). On the meaning of work: A theoretical integration and review. *Research in Organizational Behavior*, 30, 91–127.

22 Ibid. Bakker, A.B. (2010). Engagement and "job crafting": engaged employees create their own great place to work. In S. Albrecht (ed.), *Handbook of Employee Engagement: Perspectives, Issues, Research and Practice*. Edward Elgar, Cheltenham, pp. 229–44.

23 Pink, D.H. (2011). *Drive: The Surprising Truth About What Motivates Us*. Penguin, New York, NY.

24 For an introduction to the scientific definition of this construct see Edwards, J.R. (1991). Person–Job Fit: A conceptual integration, literature review, and methodological critique. In C.L. Cooper and I.T. Robertson (eds), *International Review of Industrial and Organizational Psychology* (vol. 6). John Wiley & Sons, New York, pp. 286–357; and more recently Oh, I.S., Guay, R.P., Kim, K., Harold, C.M., et al. (2014). Fit happens globally: a meta-analytic comparison of the relationships of person–environment fit dimensions with work attitudes and performance across East Asia, Europe, and North America. *Personnel Psychology*, 67(1), 99–152.

25 An increasing body of empirical studies suggest that engagement at work grows exponentially in positive gain cycles. See Salanova, M., Schaufeli, W.B., Xanthopoulou, D. and Bakker, A.B. (2010). The gain spiral of resources and work engagement: Sustaining a positive worklife. In A.B. Bakker and M.P. Leiter (eds), *Work Engagement: A Handbook of Essential Theory and Research*. Psychology Press, New York, NY, pp. 118–31.

26 See Bakker, A.B. and Bal, M.P. (2010). Weekly work engagement and performance: A study among starting teachers. *Journal of Occupational and Organizational Psychology*, 83(1), 189–206 and Bakker, A.B. (2011). An evidence-based model of work engagement. *Current Directions in Psychological Science*, 20(4), 265–69.

27 For example, Harter, J.K., Schmidt, F.L., Asplund, J.W., Killham, E.A. and Agrawal, S. (2010). Causal impact of employee work perceptions on the bottom line of organizations. *Perspectives on Psychological Science*, 5(4), 378–89; Xanthopoulou, D., Bakker, A.B., Demerouti, E. and Schaufeli, W.B. (2009). Work engagement and financial returns: A diary study on the role of job and personal resources. *Journal of Occupational and Organizational Psychology*, 82(1), 183–200.

7 Creating Career Engagement

Hitting the individual Career Sweet Spot

You can shape work experiences to create a personal "worktopia."

PASSION, PURPOSE AND CONTRIBUTION

A compelling career value proposition has to start with the personal WIFM (what's in it for me?) of each employee. Let's look at the employee perspective on creating a worktopia from a personal strategic viewpoint. How we create a worktopia for each employee has three essential components:

1   Passion

2   Purpose

3   Contribution

Passion

We define passion at work as the spark that is there when we love our work or thoroughly enjoy at least some aspects of our work. We don't expect people to be passionate about all aspects of their work all of the time, as there will always be some things we don't love as much as other aspects. We

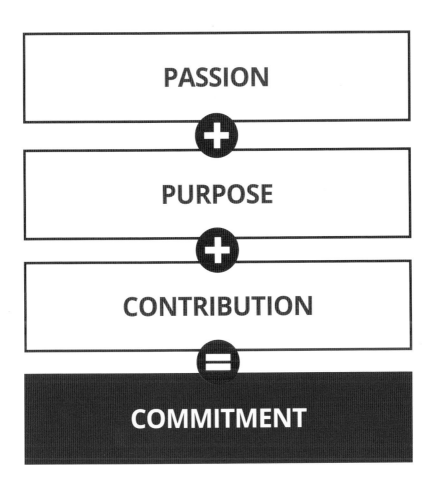

do believe, though, that it is possible to have the spark of engagement that is within every employee in your business.

There will be some facet or aspect of work that if harnessed further can lead to increased engagement. Finding that passion spark comes from:

- Aligning our **values** in some way with the organization we work with

- Having an opportunity to use our **talents** in a meaningful way, and

- When our work aligns with our personal **interests**

Where these three factors overlap is what we call an individual's sweet spot.

Where values, talents and personal interests overlap is an individual's sweet spot.

Purpose alignment

The second key factor that builds commitment from employees to the organization is purpose alignment. When your employees see how their personal mission and purpose align in some way with that of the business then your employees are significantly more likely to be committed to continued employment with you, and to want to contribute more.

Contribution

The third key factor is contribution. Your employees need to have an opportunity to contribute their skills and talents to gain a sense of adding value to the business. It is both personally satisfying and rewarding as well as having the opportunity to get reward and recognition from others for our contributions at work that make this aspect so important to motivation.

You're the happiest while you're making the greatest contribution.
— ROBERT F. KENNEDY

Tim Clark says that "contributing is different. When you contribute, the benefits don't go directly to you. They go somewhere else. Contributing is a fundamentally different driver. It takes you outside of yourself. It's not about you; it's something greater."[1]

Work engagement is defined as a "persistent, positive motivational state of fulfillment." It is when you are charged with energy and completely dedicated to your work. Being engaged is like moving up a gear. You move more quickly and your progress seems effortless.

fuel 50

So our definition of a great place to work (your own worktopia) is as follows:

- People are passionate about the work they do.

- Your employees can bring their values, talents and passions to work.

- There is purpose alignment between each of your employees and the organizational purpose.

- There is an opportunity for people to contribute their unique talents and capabilities.

- People are able to bring their best self to work — if each employee can be at their best, you will have optimum performance across the organization.

Why is passion at work so important?

You will never have engagement if you don't allow your employees to have at least a spark of passion at work. There is no question that every one of us has something that sparks our motivation and inspires us to give more, go that little bit harder. Finding that spark within each of your employees is the key to engagement.

Even for the most cynical, hard-nosed work environment out there, there will still be sparks of passion appearing. Perhaps it is the builder who takes pride in getting some detailed architraves in place, or whether it is the stockbroker who gets a tiny thrill from seeing a win for a client, or closing a day ahead of where it started. For each of us there is something that compels us to try harder and to give our best. This is the sweet spot in our work experience. Our individual, unique "worktopia."

THE CAREER SWEET SPOT

From years of coaching thousands of people to find their career sweet spot we have learnt that it is a combination of factors that consistently plays out across a career life-span. These factors may vary in importance across any one person's career, but nonetheless these factors will play out in some way. Your career sweet spot is like your career DNA, it is an undeniable part of who you are. It is the way you do things, it is the talents you have, and it is your personal passions and personality that play out in a unique way.

We see the career sweet spot like this:

**The career
sweet spot**

FIG 7.1

By combining **values**, **talents** and **passions** we can identify the career sweet spot. In effect, these three factors can provide a more systematic basis for helping employees think strategically about their careers (career shaping) and more tactically about which aspects of their current work need to be shaped to create a better fit and alignment.

Optimally, if we can shape an individual's work around these three factors, we are contributing to their work becoming more personally meaningful and purpose aligned because we are tapping into their fundamental values, their innate talents and potential and their personal passions.

Let's look at each of these factors in more detail.

VALUES ALIGNMENT

Business reports cite a perceived mismatch between employee values and working conditions as principal reasons for leaving, especially during the first year of tenure. Some 52% of overall attrition occurs in the first year of employment, due to "poor fit between individual and organizational values" (37%) and "missed expectations of duties/or schedule" (30%). Interestingly, "lack of direct possibilities for advancement" predicted only 12% of first-year attrition.[2]

The related concept of "embeddedness," which refers to compatibility of values between the individual and the organization, as well as valued social contact and networks, has been shown to interact with job engagement to determine intention to quit.[3]

We always start with values, because this is a fundamental to who we are at work. If you are values aligned at work, you have a greater chance of delivering your best work. You will have a stronger belief in what you do, and a greater chance of being purpose aligned where you will gain a sense of fulfillment and a greater sense of satisfaction at work.

We define values in two ways — personal values and career values.

- **Personal values** are those fundamental "non-negotiables" to who you are and how you do things at work. Typically, these will be highly visible to other people. Whether you are driven by expertise, passion or kindness, if you are truly living your personal values at work these things will be evident to others. They are part of your DNA, as real and individual as your fingerprints.

- **Career values** are our non-negotiable career success factors. They will be the things that we need and crave in our work. Career values include a wide range of things ranging from people contact, teamwork, through to a sense of results or even fun and excitement at work. These career values are the blueprint for defining your career sweet spot in a simple and tactical way, allowing us to gain engagement benefits.

Personal values

Firstly, let's look more closely at personal values. If we were to look at someone like Richard Branson, most of us would agree that he embodies values and qualities such as far-sightedness and adventurousness. Mark Zuckerburg's values seem to speak of entrepreneurialism and dedication.

Our personal values are fundamentally important. While many of us may not be able to articulate exactly what is most important to us, any careful observer or close friend will be able to give you an idea of what they see as your most closely held personal values. If you think of someone close to you and try to guess their top three values you will probably be not far off. If I look at my "other half," a true fitness fanatic, I would describe his top values as self-discipline, persistence and focused determination to achieve a goal. And because he is also CEO of a global organization it is not surprising that these same values permeate their business culture.

If we look at the people we each most admire, we can get a glimpse of our true aspirational values. These values may represent who we want to become or could be in the future.

In essence, our values will always be a work in progress. They will be something that underpins the way we live our lives, and conduct ourselves at work and elsewhere. It's a good idea to take stock of what your underlying values are. The more we accept them and share them with others the stronger they will become.

Values will be fundamental to our personal brands, and personal reputation will become increasingly important as we live in an increasingly social world on a global scale.

Values are fundamental to our goal alignment at work; they will underpin everything we do. It is about the choices that we make on a daily and weekly basis. We find that values become increasingly important the further someone is on in their career. In the early stages of our careers, our first decisions are often made around our talents, because that is what is visible to others. As an example, a school leaver who is great at math may be encouraged to become an accountant or actuary, whereas another student has great verbal skills and has a talent for debate, and so gets feedback from others that she would make a great lawyer. However, our values may be more subtle and less visible to others, yet they can have a significant influence on our career decision making.

Values alignment: the fastest way to build employee engagement

Values and purpose-aligned work is associated with numerous organization benefits including increased job satisfaction, motivation and performance.[4] But is it really possible to have true values alignment at work? Many companies we work with will have espoused values on the wall that their employees may or may not be able to recite accurately. However, if we were to ask via a survey what values the company actually lives by day to day we may get a completely different story.

Values alignment at work enables us to feel more satisfied and fulfilled, and according to Daniel Pink a sense of purpose at work will be more motivational than money.[5] A sense of shared purpose will align people more effectively than dollar rewards — just think of the discretionary effort that is delivered when you have purpose alignment at work.

Values and purpose-aligned work is associated with numerous organization benefits including increased job satisfaction, motivation and performance.

The benefits of purpose-aligned work

Supporting your managers to have conversations with their team around the alignment between individual and organizational goals will have multiple pay-offs:

- Managers will understand what motivates each team member.

- Team members will understand where their colleagues are coming from and know where they will be most motivated to contribute added value to the team. This may be, for example, by being the person adding fun and humor, or the person doing the support and appreciation by bringing in the baking — it can all add value to team performance and harmony in the long run.

PURPOSE ALIGNMENT CASE STUDY

Frucor, an Australian Best Places to Work winner two years running, ran purpose alignment workshops across the organization, using values alignment exercises as a core part of these workshops. Everyone across the business was involved from blue-collar line workers to the CEO. The goal set down by the head of OD was to create a program to connect each employee's personal values, purpose and vision to that of the business.

There are many definitions of personal purpose and much written on the topic. Debbie Schultz, OD Strategist with Fuel50, elaborates: "Our first step was to define purpose for people, then provide some powerful questions to help each person decode this for themselves, including insight questions about passions and motivators. This also included questions directly relating to the unique contribution each person brings, such as 'What is achieved because I am here? And what would not happen if I was not here?'"

During a one-day workshop employees were supported through a process to join the dots from personal values, vision and purpose to that of the business through self-reflection, leader-led team discussions and powerful facilitation. The results speak for themselves — of the respondents to the post-program survey, 80% had an increased understanding of their own values and personal purpose, coupled with 91% increased understanding of their connection to the organization's purpose and strategy, with 83% agreeing they now have a better understanding of the unique contribution that they make to the business.

Debbie further notes that "Anecdotal feedback was even more powerful, with this program regarded as one of the best training programs ever. Managers across the organization felt that the conversations this program sparked were like gold dust to the business, in that they were able to tap into the real drivers of personal performance for each employee."

- If each team member has a sense of how their personal values align with those of the organization, there is a stronger sense of cohesion and purpose.

When there is purpose alignment in a team there will be real power in the collective effort, which will mean that more will be achieved. There is real benefit in taking time to understand individual and collective values at work.

In our experience, it will be very rare, if not impossible, for someone not to have at least one area of alignment with the team and organization's values. Moreover, according to Berg et al., "the design of employees' jobs can significantly shape how they experience the meaningfulness of their work . . . work that employees believe is significant in that it serves an important purpose."[6]

We inevitably come to the conclusion that a group of people come together and exist as an institution that we call a company so that they are able to accomplish something collectively that they could not accomplish separately — they make a contribution to society, a phrase which sounds trite but which is fundamental.

— DAVID PACKARD, CO-FOUNDER OF HEWLETT-PACKARD, 1939

fuel
50

Work shaping and values

In the workplace, understanding your employees' values will help create a more rewarding and fulfilling work experience for them. By understanding the top five personal and career values of your team members a manager can easily make micro changes in the job and work that may have a significant impact on job satisfaction. These potentially quick wins can have an immediate effect and give the employee a sense of "architecting" their own employment experience, with a significant impact on career satisfaction, individual engagement, motivation and performance.

Let's see how this works. Jane, for example, has top work values of expertise and appreciation. It is quite easy for her manager, by understanding these, to create opportunities for Jane to share her knowledge and expertise with others in the business, and to give her public accolades for her contributions.

 Find out what the values are of your people and you will be able to go a long way towards building employee loyalty.[7]

Look at the following value examples and suggested alignment tweaks, most of which cost nothing but which will be incredibly rewarding and motivating to that individual.

CAREER VALUE	LEADER TIP
Challenge	Provide stretch assignment, give project work that provides challenge.
Expertise	Find out what area of expertise they most want to develop, provide learning opportunities, buddy with someone with that expertise.
Appreciation	Make sure you regularly thank these individuals and publicly or privately acknowledge their input. A simple thank-you card for those motivated by appreciation will go a long way.
Professional reputation	Help these individuals to get their work published, receive public acknowledgements, and endorsements on LinkedIn; allow them to attend networking meetings or speak at conferences.

All of these actions are simple, but each of the small changes will directly impact the satisfaction of your employee. *You light the fire one person at a time, but you can start a bushfire* if you enable all your managers to have these conversations with each of their team members.

TALENTS AND THE SWEET SPOT

The second key factor in defining a career sweet spot for your employees is talent. Talents are those innate abilities that we have, and often if we have them they are irrepressible.

What we refer to as talents is what Mary Ann Bopp at IBM refers to as expertise. This is the amalgamation of your competencies (common to all employees and key indicators for success in high-performing individuals), skills (specific to role requirements or for aspirational roles), and capabilities (skills, experiences and expertise that result in capabilities as valued by clients) or what Berg et al. refer to as strengths or "areas of talent that can be productively applied at work."[8]

Talents can be both natural and learned. Many of us may once have hated public speaking, but when we become more skilled, find that we grow to love it and others would then describe it as a talent.

Hidden talents can represent untapped potential for an organization. In our experience most people have talents that are not being fully utilized. Take our own HR Intern, Cam, fresh from university with a passion for HR. Turns out he was a global gaming champion in his younger days, much to his parents' concern at the time. We believe they would be surprised to find that we now have given him a project to review the gamification of our online career engagement tools — who better to understand how to do it than someone who has had the skills and passion, and was using those skills for fun?

Over years of running career boot camps, we have seen many administrative staff, or production line workers, who have great talents that are not being leveraged fully at work. It may be the blue-collar worker who is a church leader with well-developed speaking and influence skills, or the payroll person who has a hidden talent for systems and organizing things. These are natural talents that can be further utilized, which will have pay-off for both your employees in terms of personal satisfaction and for the business by tapping into the discretionary effort that underlies engagement.

Talents and work shaping

So talents are the keys to making the tactical work-shaping changes that will impact engagement. This is where we link to one of the three core facets identified in the work-shaping principles above of task shaping. Tasks can typically be shaped in three ways (according to Berg et al.): [9]

- Adding tasks — adding activities or projects that play to one's talents or align to an interest area.

- Emphasizing tasks — by allocating more time, energy and attention to them.

- Redesigning tasks — finding ways to re-engineer existing tasks to make them more meaningful. For example, the dental hygienist who focuses on education not just teeth cleaning.

So using more of our talents at work is necessary for our work satisfaction and for organizational engagement. People can become frustrated if they see things occurring when they would have liked to have made a contribution towards an outcome.

fuel
50

Giving people a sense of adding value or contribution to the business is pivotal to engagement. Talent actualization will help deliver more discretionary effort from each employee, and it taps into additional skills and talents, allowing employees to make a greater contribution.

PASSION AND THE CAREER SWEET SPOT

Your preferences and passions make up the third factor that contributes to your career sweet spot. We all have things that interest us, and it is these interests that contribute to our work preferences and our personal passions. Work shaping, in ways that create opportunities to pursue passions or the activities and topics that spark deep interest, can be a valuable source of personal reward, engagement and meaningfulness.[10]

The Holland Codes
We consider that psychologist John Holland's (1969) model for understanding work preferences still holds a lot of value. Holland hypothesized that work interests align to our personality preferences, and his research shows that there are typically six interest areas that combine to create personal work interest preferences. The Holland Codes or the Holland Occupational Themes (RIASEC) is based upon six personality types: Thinkers, Doers, Helpers, Persuaders, Creators, Organizers. Each letter or code stands for a particular "type": Realistic (Doers), Investigative (Thinkers), Artistic (Creators), Social (Helpers), Enterprising (Persuaders), and Conventional (Organizers).[11]

According to the Committee on Scientific Awards, Holland's "research shows that personalities seek out and flourish in career environments they fit and that jobs and career environments are classifiable by the personalities that flourish in them." It also shows that your choice of work can be an expression of your personality. Holland himself acknowledged that "a six-category scheme built on the assumption that there are only six kinds of people in the world is unacceptable on the strength of common sense alone. But a six-category scheme that allows a simple ordering of a person's resemblance to each of the six models provides the possibility of 720 different personality patterns."

PERSONAL CHALLENGE

Imagine you were meeting a friend outside Barnes & Noble and you just had a message to say that they were running 20 minutes late. You decide to go in and browse the bookstore while you are waiting. Which section do you go to first and second, and why?

There will be clues to your interests in the sections you go to, so if you are attracted to the celeb magazines perhaps your interest in people is at play. Or if you go straight to the business books, it might be your interest in economics, entrepreneurialism or leadership is the attraction here.

What are the underlying interests that are at play in your own career? Also pay attention to what interests and latent passions might be evident in your colleagues and staff. Maybe even try the personal challenge question (above) on your employees — you never know what hidden talent you might discover.

Interests drive learning

Our interests drive our learning. So just as we may have wandered into a bookstore and browsed a topic area, our interests determine what we stop to read on the internet, or what we stop to watch when channel-surfing on the TV. It is these lifelong learning moments that grow from our interests and build into an area of expertise and knowledge that makes us uniquely marketable. Even if it is always the sports channel that you are drawn to, there can be pay-offs. A newly hired salesperson of ours has an impressive knowledge of all sports and manages to connect with nearly every single prospect with his ability to share a knowledge and interest in the sporting interests of the people he talks to. He is a legendary rapport builder and is effectively leveraging his passions and interests in a high pay-off way.

Of course, our learning is not just about these casual learning moments; it is the structured learning that we have invested in which becomes our expertise base. It is as relevant for the mechanic who becomes fascinated with hydraulics or electronics as for the accountant with an interest in foreign exchange rates or asset utilization. These targeted learning experiences add significantly to our career capital asset base, as discussed earlier.

As we have already mentioned, 86% of people have talents that are not being fully utilized by their employers, and more than 75% of people want to contribute more to their employers. Tapping into the hidden passions in your people will have engagement, performance and productivity benefits.

Increasingly, we hear from the businesses that we talk to that employees want opportunities that align with their interests. They are hungry to understand how they can take their passions and talents and leverage them within the business. Many of the organizations we work with struggle to provide these opportunities. Using technology enablers can support this in a self-sustaining way, delivering "socially enabled" real employee stories as to what they love about their work, what competencies are required and what they would recommend to someone who might be interested in that role. This approach is becoming increasingly evident in those organizations that are leading the way in career management practices and who are delivering the most compelling career value propositions.

NOTES

1   Clark, T. (2012). *The Employee Engagement Mindset*. McGraw-Hill, New York, NY.

2   These statistics were published by Talentkeepers (2013). Retrieved from: www.
    talentkeepers.com/download/2013-TalentKeepers-Employee-Engagement-
    Retention-Trends-Report-Final.pdf.

3   Mitchell, T. R., Holtom, B.C., Lee, T.W., Sablynski, C.J. and Erez, M. (2001). Why
    people stay: Using job embeddedness to predict voluntary turnover. *Academy
    of Management Journal*, 44(6), 1102–21; Crossley, C.D., Bennett, R.J., Jex, S.M. and
    Burnfield, J.L. (2007). Development of a global measure of job embeddedness
    and integration into a traditional model of voluntary turnover. *Journal of Applied
    Psychology*, 92(4), 1031.

4   See Grant, A.M. (2007). Relational job design and the motivation to make a
    prosocial difference. *Academy of Management Review*, 32(2), 393–417; Hackman, J.R.
    and Oldham, G.R. (1980). *Work Redesign*. Addison-Wesley, Reading, Massachusetts;
    Rosso, B.D., Dekas, K.H. and Wrzesniewski, A. (2010). On the meaning of work: A
    theoretical integration and review. *Research in Organizational Behavior*, 30, 91–127.

5   Pink, D.H. (2011). *Drive: The Surprising Truth About What Motivates Us*. Penguin, New
    York, NY.

6   Berg, J.M., Dutton, J.E. and Wrzesniewski, A. (2008). What is job crafting and why
    does it matter? Retrieved from: http://positiveorgs.bus.umich.edu/wp-content/
    uploads/What-is-Job-Crafting-and-Why-Does-it-Matter1.pdf.

7   Chalofsky, N.E. (2010). *Meaningful Workplaces: Reframing How and Where We Work*.
    John Wiley and Sons, San Francisco.

8   Berg, Dutton and Wrzesniewski (2013), op. cit.

9   Berg, Dutton and Wrzesniewski (2013), op. cit.

10 Rosso, Dekas and Wrzesniewski (2010), op. cit.

11 Holland, J.L., Whitney, D.R., Cole, N.S. and Richards, J.M., Jr. (1969). *An Empirical
    Occupational Classification Derived from a Theory of Personality and Intended for
    Practice and Research* (ACT Research Report No. 29). American College Testing
    Program, Iowa City, IA; Holland, J.L. (1996). Exploring careers with a typology: What
    we have learned and some new directions. *American Psychologist*, 51(4), 397.

8 | The Pathway Challenge

The challenge is about creating meaningful and inspirational pathways.

HOW DO WE FORGE A CAREER PATH?

A core premise of this book is the need for each individual to have a workplace where they can fulfill their career drivers on a daily basis. We have seen this in action across tens of thousands of employees, as they apply what is important to them to their current job. Chapter 6 on work shaping highlights how each individual, supported by a manager who is proactive and mindful of career engagement, can create a working environment that hits critical career sweet spots each day.

However, what we also know is that having clarity around your career path is the next piece of the career engagement puzzle. People want to know what their future might be with their organization, what types of role they could achieve and how to make that a reality.

Having clarity around your career path is the next piece of the career engagement puzzle.

Hence the challenge. As we know, the future is ever shifting and certainty of job roles is a rarity. For most of the organizations we work with, pathways to various roles are changing constantly, and as our talent needs shift and grow, we must create new pathways that build the competencies and experience we need to meet future business needs. What was a clear pathway yesterday is not today — broken by role deconstruction or right-sizing, mergers and acquisitions and business change, as well as past pathway irrelevancy to future business need.

Historically, career pathways have been defined by hierarchical or ladder-based organizational structures. We moved from entry level to senior to management to executive, all within our immediate job neighborhood. We knew the next step, because typically there was only one way to go, and that was to our manager's role. Our view of a career was limited by what we saw each day: our colleague's jobs, our manager's job and their manager's role. Our blinkers were firmly on — we could only see what was directly in front of us, and we were constrained by the reins of the organization. Ultimately, the employer chose our path. These traditional career pathways implies a right way and a wrong way to career management. The right way is defined and supported by the organization, with clearly marked ladder career movements that allow for minimal individualization.

This is limiting in a number of ways. A linear and restricted view of career progression:

- Prevents cross-silo fertilization of ideas and knowledge

- Presumes that the only valid development pathway is "up"

- Is based on the premise that progression is only possible within one area of knowledge, so you are restricted to your current business cohort

Although these reporting line career pathways are still valid, our clients are telling us that they want to offer greater variety and cross-functional movement within their organization.

 They want to create variety for employees, reduce risk of business unit isolation and improve business agility and decision making, and to build broader and more diverse capability on the talent bench.

Creating this shift within a typical business built on hierarchical progression, leadership pathways and talent "trapping" within functional areas requires a tactical and strategic approach.

With this in mind, this chapter will focus on two key areas:

- Employee-driven career pathing

- Organization-driven career pathing to meet succession and talent needs for the future

Customized pathway mapping for each individual, based on their own needs and career drivers, is essential to building motivating employee pathways. A one-size-fits-all approach doesn't work for all, as we know, so it is essential that each employee's career pathway is as unique as they are.

Typically, career pathways are documented and created by the organization. Having this clarity around historical pathway movements and role-based succession pipelines is a career engagement hygiene factor that is a foundation for employee exploration. However, how someone navigates the organization and builds their own path should be unique to that individual, leveraging their particular experiences and talents and allowing them to add greater value to the organization. Instead of choosing a path from the map in front of you, employees need to create a unique pathing map that activates and builds individual and organizational value each step of the way.

Note two concepts here:

- The map is a forecast (susceptible to change and needing recalibration regularly)

- The individual builds it step by step, shaping each step along the way with a focus on talent actualization and experience management.

Clarity of career purpose

Educating and supporting employees to create a personal career map is integral to the success of this approach. Creating a personal career purpose and vision (how you want to execute that purpose over the longer term) is the first step for individuals creating a career pathing map. As Dan Pink talks about in his book Drive, we have a natural need to contribute to something bigger than ourselves.[1] The first step in supporting your employees to create valid career pathways is giving them the opportunity to create clarity around the type of career they want to build and the reasons for doing so. This understanding of personal purpose and vision can then be applied to the immediate role that person is undertaking and can help direct next career steps. Future roles are not dictated by organization hierarchy, but instead by opportunities to see purpose played out at work.

Leveraging passions and talents

Helping employees identify and leverage talents and passions in their career map is the next step in helping them choose opportunities which fulfill their vision and purpose today and in the future.

What you like to do plays an important part in defining future career steps in pathways. Career pathing needs to move away from an "organizational chart" approach and instead, for each individual, start from their passions and purpose. Understanding what I love to do and am passionate about is a better indicator of a satisfying career pathway than simply looking at roles that are directly linked to my own via a manager on the organizational chart.

Our passions or interests are useful in career pathways for a number of reasons:

- They help direct our search for roles. Interest plays a large part in job satisfaction. If a job meets your interests you are likely to enjoy it; so, not surprisingly, interests can account for a large part of finding the right career pathway. Many people, faced with career decisions, find it difficult to focus on particular areas. It's also impossible to learn about every type of work that exists within an organization. By narrowing our research to roles that fit our interest, we are condensing our search but not shutting out areas that we might find rewarding and enjoyable.

- Our interests inspire us to go the extra mile, invest discretionary effort and learn. This is helpful when considering sideways moves where we may need to step outside our field of expertise to apply our skills in new functional interests.

- Passion builds talent and experience. As noted above, if we are interested in something, it is easier to spend more time doing that thing or learning about it. This way we are building our knowledge and skill-set — and talents.

Where talents and passions align, we have a great motivational fit — that sweet spot described in Chapter 7. So it makes sense to focus on pathways that leverage our talents and satisfy our interests. This combination might be in roles that we haven't considered in the past, or in areas that are new.

Each career path stepping stone should more fully leverage talents and passions and take us that much closer to fulfilling our vision and living our purpose. These steps don't need to be hierarchical; the lattice approach described below can sometimes be a faster way to activate passion and purpose.

Enabling lattice vs ladder movement

Hierarchical or ladder career movement is easy enough to facilitate as an organization. The promotee often has been accepted by the promoter as an easy successor, they have the functional experience and knowledge and face validity to perform in the role, and "know the ways things are done." The promotee has to manage challenges such as team management of previous colleagues, but largely they are seen as a "slam dunk" for the role.

Over is the new up! 🗲🗲
— JOANNE CLEAVER

New hires from outside the department, in contrast, are much more difficult to facilitate. Resistance to those without functional experience can be high from the existing team, and there may be a learning period as the individual comes up to speed with transactional skills and competencies.

So why create ripples in what seems to be a very calm pond? If we have enough people wanting the vacant role inside the team, why open things up to employees from other functions — particularly if it is going to be harder for the new team member and our existing team? Conversely, why would we want to encourage great team members to exit our own team to join another?

The reality is that we often don't have the people in our own team ready to step up, and managers who don't support talent growth lose them.

Why lattice?

The lattice refers to multi-directional career pathways that cross functions, teams and areas of expertise. A lattice career can be demonstrated by someone who has moved across the organization, potentially taking lower or same-level roles to gain experience. This zigzagging approach is focused on exploring, broadening experience, and applying transferable skills in new functional areas.

 We believe lattice career pathing contributes to short and long-term organizational success by broadening talent contribution and access, and supports greater organization transparency, advocacy and execution.

Consider the following:

Talent trapping vs talent banking

Talent trapping refers to the practice where managers hold talent within their team or function, discouraging that individual from moving roles or progressing and actively withholding career advocacy across the organization. This has short-term gains in that the talented employee continues to boost the team's performance and makes the manager's life easier.

We have all had great employees who make our jobs a dream, people we have invested in heavily to get them to that level. However, at some point and usually sooner than expected, if not provided with career opportunities that individual will exit the organization to achieve career growth and development. Even worse, that talented individual may stay in the team, but becomes disillusioned and may engage in derailing behaviors.

The positive alternative to talent trapping is talent banking, which is an organizational strategy that contributes to better management of talent. Talent is instead "banked" by the organization as an organization asset (not a manager-owned or team-specific asset). They are given the opportunity to fulfill potential across a multitude of teams and environments, creating exponential returns to the organization. These individuals can hold roles of reasonable tenure, but are carefully watched to ensure that they are maximizing their potential and are not limiting the value they can add.

Talent can be banked as an organization asset. Employees are given the opportunity to fulfill potential across a multitude of teams and environments.

Lattice career movement provides additional opportunities to make talent banking happen. Talent is not restricted by hierarchical opportunities but instead can increase career capability across the organization, increasing their own personal value and the value they add to the business. Employees can add value across the entire organization, utilizing competency in new areas of the business. They can grow new team members' thinking and commercial insight as well as building broader experience for themselves.

This encourages an organizational view of goal achievement as opposed to just a team-based approach.

Note, it is important that lateral opportunities are not restricted to just what lateral moves have occurred in the past or what leaders consider possible. With the exception of essential industry or field-required qualifications, recruitment and selection thinking should be as open and broad as possible. Allowing for reasoned "wild card" moves supports individual and organizational agility, diversity and transformational career experiences.

Better talent bench strength

Talented people often move rapidly up the hierarchical ladder early in their career. The potential and success of these individuals is identified early and during times of business growth will be accelerated. This can be great in terms of talent engagement but can result in mid to senior-level individuals who have resulting skill-sets and competencies that are shallow and relatively untested. Lattice career moves allow challenge and movement, but also the opportunity to deepen core competencies. Testing your decisions, interactions and execution at a similar level but in a different environment can round out any unformed edges and provide a better foundation for business challenges.

Creating agile career mindsets for leaders and employees

Roles in organizations are constantly changing and morphing, and some jobs that are predominant now barely existed 20 years ago. Consider the analyst roles in your organizations; many of them were unheard of 20 years ago, and they have emerged as technology has evolved. Lateral moves help individuals to stay marketable and agile in changing workplaces and creates a workforce that can ebb and flow as business demands change.

Openness by the leader, in terms of where talent might come from, supports greater team diversity, positively challenges team dynamics and creates variety in thought and approach.

Supporting individuals to activate lateral career pathways helps them and the organization to achieve the above outcomes. It also truly creates a customized career proposition, led by that individual and evident as they move across and up the organization and not just directly up.

All of these factors combine to create an employee-led career pathway. It is one where the employees are clearly in the driver's seat, and the organization responds dynamically to facilitate such progress, clearly benefiting by increased employee agility, engagement and discretionary effort. A "career lattice" mentality allows for greater freedom of choice, and firmly places career ownership in the hands of the employee. It makes sense, then, that career pathing also sits there.

ORGANIZATION-DRIVEN CAREER PATHING TO MEET SUCCESSION AND FUTURE TALENT NEEDS

With all this individual actualization, does the organization still have a role in communicating career pathways?

Organization's role

In two key areas, the organization has a critical role.

Firstly, as a provider of information. Presenting sample pathway possibilities in terms of career movements sparks employee and manager action, and encourages discussion. Organizations often hold role data in a central place and need to communicate this to employees. It is tricky to think of lateral moves, after all, if you have no idea what roles exist in your organization!

Secondly, by creating alternatives to traditional pathways that maximize organizational and individual return. What we are describing here is an agile approach to career pathing owned by the employee and facilitated by the organization. We all know about role-based career pathing — pathways which are based on linked roles and seem common sense. They are still important, but there is an opportunity for organizations to build value-adding pathways that deliver to both individual and organizational need. The following describes some pathway alternatives driven by the organization.

Leader vs expert pathways

Leadership pathways are often clearly articulated and understood, supported by leadership programs and high potential initiatives. Leaders who have achieved senior levels of success are often those who are responsible for critical business areas and manage at the highest level of the organization. They are visible, well known and have status. This can be aspirational for those following in their footsteps, but presents a challenge for individuals who are equally talented but are not a fit for people or functional management.

Nurturing expert pathways is essential to retaining core staff, but it is often overlooked. Providing high status expert pathways allows your expert talent to continue to grow within your organization and achieve higher profile and remuneration. Expert pathways could include such additional responsibilities as:

- Industry representation

- Challenging, high profile or choice assignments

- Mentoring of others

- Providing input to critical business decisions

- The opportunity to move laterally into other areas at senior levels

By making these pathway options visible and attractive as leadership pathways, your organization has greater appeal to your experts and provides aspirational targets for experts' careers.

Career pathways as diversity enablers

We talked briefly about allowing for reasoned wild card moves and we will expand on that here. Essentially, this is about increasing diversity of team dynamic, thought and contribution.

Supporting leaders to see potential in non-typical internal applicants can help remove some barriers to cross-functional recruitment. This might be through highlighting additional benefits brought to the team by someone with a different CV than anticipated. Weighting factors such as behavioral competencies, new (to the team) internal relationships and exposure to alternative company perspectives may mean an external (to that team) candidate becomes more attractive than someone from within the existing team. Seeing how this person can immediately add value, albeit in a different way, may support the manager to make the decision to bring this person on board.

As organizations increasingly become competitive for talent, this may be forced anyway. There might not be anyone available in the existing team or externally with the exact experiential set, resulting in a need to bring in potential as opposed to experience. It seems sensible to start this shift in mindset early, so leaders are already well versed in spotting great employees — despite atypical CVs.

This approach naturally breeds diversity and opens the door for individuals who may have had difficulty joining specific teams in the past due to lack of traditional experience.

 These lateral and wild card pathways, supported and endorsed by the organization, are an alternative to the typical organizational chart pathway approach.

fuel 50

Succession pathways

These are critical role pathways, developing individuals for specific positions within the organization. They might be two to three roles deep, and are often linked to specific individuals within the organizations, earmarked for senior roles.

These pathways are unique, in that they are often built by the organization as opposed to being employee driven. The trick to making them work is communication and transparency. As these pathways can take years to eventuate for the individual, and may be road-blocked by other, more senior talent, ongoing dialogue is critical. It might be that lateral experiential-driven moves are encouraged during the wait to ensure ongoing motivation and challenge are delivered to the individual waiting.

Critical experience pathways

Organizations also have a clear need to build competency and experience for projected skill gaps and to achieve business goals. Providing an alternative from the job title-led career pathway to an experience-led agile career pathway model allows the individual to direct their path to roles which build specific experience sets. The agility comes from the individual actively choosing roles that deliver these experiences and being cognizant of the fact that the roles which deliver this may differ over time. For example, a finance role during a recession builds different experience sets than a finance role during an acquisition.

Regularly communicating the experience and competencies required by the organization for the business as it stands today, for critical projects and for the future, allows individuals to make informed career path decisions. These decisions will support a matched portfolio, helping them stay more marketable. For the organization, it builds stronger staff strength and agility to meet future business growth or challenges.

Shared stories of how individual employees have developed an experience-led career pathway can be useful to demonstrate this to others.

In the 2020 workplace, the old linear pathways are almost impossible to construct as they are job and task led as opposed to recognizing individual employee traits and potential and building critical experience.

Reconstructing how we approach pathways is critical to keeping the pathways concept relevant while still delivering aspirational targets for staff. Career pathway management and communication need to take a step up from job linking — and instead be agile, business-need relevant and provide an aspirational target for each person regardless of their career wants and needs. The pathway challenge for each organization is about creating meaningful and inspirational pathways. These pathways will be owned by each person, clearly linked to individual purpose and create talent actualization employees who are as passionate about their current role as they are about the next step.

 Career pathway management and communication need to be agile, relevant to business needs and provide an aspirational target for each person regardless of their career wants and needs.

NOTES

1   Pink, D.H. (2011). *Drive: The Surprising Truth About What Motivates Us*. Penguin, New York, NY.

PART C

Best Practice Organizational Principles for Career Engagement

CREATING THE CAREER ENGAGEMENT MASTER PLAN

9 The Pillars of Career Engagement in Organizations

The vision: workplaces in the twenty-second century where everyone is 100% engaged.

Leaders, managers and HR are increasingly seeking new ways to create a high-performing workforce, and with higher percentages of knowledge workers, this is becoming increasingly complex. Helping individual employees map their personal career passion and purpose to their current job and employer, while tapping into their motivated talents, is a powerful way to generate discretionary effort and create greater employee career engagement.

Today it's all about engagement and how well a company is able to inspire its employees. Best-practice organizations want to create an environment that facilitates and enables people to use and express their full complement of talents. By allowing employees to bring more of their talents to work and align their purpose and values, modern workplaces are looking to increase their level of engagement.

fuel 50

Career engagement occurs when capability, compatibility, contribution and communication are combined.

Capability + Compatibility + Contribution + Communication = Career Engagement

The mutual career engagement across these four factors isn't created by one activity or project alone. Instead it is a multi-faceted initiative — a symphony of business, manager and individual actions that all work together to create a career-engaged workforce. These actions can be launched in clusters or over time to create ease of execution, but they must work together to create perfect music!

This chapter introduces some practical models of how to create this symphony and how the principles discussed in previous chapters work within your organizational context. In particular, we introduce three models that work together to form a career engagement strategy for your business:

- The four foundational pillars of career engagement (the 4 C's)

- The three levels of career engagement (the 3 E's)

- The employee life-cycle

The vision of 100% engagement includes an alignment and powerful synergy of individual and corporate purpose.

We believe that, just around the corner, there is a new way of working. We see a world where people are purpose aligned, bringing a vast and diverse range of talents to pull together for some common good as an organization. That re-imagined workplace needs to fully leverage the talents of each individual and allow the shaping and refashioning of a work experience that plays to the talents of each person and allows people the freedom to work in a way that is best for them and equally contributes to business outcomes.

The essence of this can be distilled in four key pillars: capability, compatibility, contribution, and communication. These pillars are the core functions of your career engagement strategy. Each of them plays out in different ways for each employee and leader, and they need to be supported by the frameworks of the organization at every turn. You can read more about these four pillars of engagement in our research paper on global career management best practices (2014).[1]

For the purposes of translating these pillars into guidelines for organizational career management best practices, a brief description of each is given below.

Capability

- Leveraging the capability and talent within each and every employee is key to a high performance 2020 workplace. If each employee can play to their best talents, and have an opportunity to grow and extend their motivated talents, you will inevitably have an organization that is also playing its best game.

- We use the words game and play deliberately, because when everyone's talents are fully leveraged work should also be fun.

- People are focused and adding exponential value by bringing their best game to work.

Compatibility

- Alignment of goals, values and purpose is critical in the creation of a best place to work environment. It is the organizational responsibility to build alignment between the individual goals and the organizational goals. Where there is alignment of goals, missions and objectives between the individual and the business you will be creating the foundation for high performance and high engagement. This alignment is a key to allowing people the work freedom to bring their best selves to work.

- Open career discussions increase alignment between underlying values, and they ensure that the employee and the organization are on the same page. This results in a sense of fit and belonging, as well as the satisfaction that arises when we are able to express our values at work.

- Long-term goal alignment allows the individual to see how their daily efforts relate to the broader organizational mission, and creates a win–win situation where both parties work in tandem to achieve their mutual goals.

Contribution

- Creating a mindset across the entire organization where everyone is adding just that bit more value, thinking about what they can do better, is the hallmark of highly engaged employees and the best places to work organizations these people want to work in.

- With the right tools you can create opportunities for everyone to contribute more and to create a sense of personal success and satisfaction based on that contribution. You increase your chances of keeping these people performing at a higher level and retaining them for longer.

- Clarity of how your contribution is valued by the organization is also key to this pillar, and transparency of how your individual activity contributes to the wider business is essential.

Communication

- Best places to work have great dialogue between leaders and their people. Leaders are enabled to grow the career capability of employees through powerful conversations. Your people can clearly see the opportunities and the people that can help them.

- Memorable career moments are delivered when you have a leader who asks the right questions and who supports your personal career success — whatever that means to you — and therein lies the secret of the Fuel50 program.

- For individuals it means defining what that success looks like to you, sharing the insights with the right people and creating a plan to make it happen that is easy to actualize. For leaders, it is about creating opportunity to discuss career aspirations regularly and ensuring that you provide plenty of opportunity for work shaping so that your employees can leverage their motivated talents at work, be more goal aligned and more motivated to contribute more.

 These four foundational pillars play across three different layers of your career engagement strategy.

THE THREE LEVELS OF CAREER ENGAGEMENT (3 E'S) ACROSS THE EMPLOYEE LIFE-CYCLE

Within your career engagement strategy are three tiers of initiative at play.

- **Individual empowerment**: Enabling individuals to understand key career drivers, create a motivating career pathway linked to their current role, and create goals that are aligned to their values and aspirations

- **Leader enablement**: Supporting managers to have easy but meaningful career conversations with their people that are delivered across three levels of career engagement coaching

- **Organizational effectiveness**: Enabling your organization to have a clear line of sight to staff career drivers, succession risk areas and engagement levers to support strategic people initiatives and business success

Let's take a look at how these factors interplay to create a career engagement workplace (from the perspective of a staff member). The 12-box Career Engagement Grid that follows shows how each of the 4 C's is perceived by an individual with an organization, along with the corresponding interventions that have led to these outcomes.

4 C's	3 E's		
	Individual empowerment:	Leader enablement:	Organizational effectiveness:
Capability	I bring my best "game" to work, leveraging my motivated talents and building new capability each day, starting from my current role. I am aware of, and ready to step into, stretch opportunities and new roles that fit my own career goals as well as fulfilling organizational need.	My leader has the mandate to manage his/her team's tasks and workflow to create success opportunities for individual team members.	My organization has a clear line of sight to employee motivated talents available to fulfill critical roles and succession pipelines and targeted programs to reduce talent gaps.
Compatibility	I live my values at work and feel aligned to the direction of the business. I understand and am passionate about my organization's goals and objectives.	My leader regularly communicates and advocates for organizational purpose and values, and encourages me to communicate how my own aspirations and values map to these.	As well as my performance and potential, my aspirations are also understood and mapped by the organization to high potential programs and succession pipelines. Staff regularly refer friends/family to this organization as employer, reinforcing our great workplace feel.

Contribution	I add value to my organization each and every day. I know my input and work is important and I find opportunities in my daily work to go the extra mile.	My leader engages and rewards me in business-as-usual activities and special projects that leverage my unique mix of career drivers and aspirations and build current and future career success within my current role and business unit, my organization and my industry.	My career pathway within my organization is not just restricted to hierarchical leadership roles. Instead I have choices including expert pathways, lateral/career moves and cross-functional opportunities. My organizational experience and knowledge have the potential to be leveraged in agile ways.
Communication	Conversations with my manager about my career wants and needs, aspirations and goals are an ongoing part of my employee experience — and started from onboarding. I have access to additional mentors and coaches, and these conversations are seen as enriching my relationship with my current manager — instead of challenging it.	My leader knows my career aspirations and goals and regularly discusses progress and achievements with me. My leader advocates for me across my organization, supporting me to build my career and add organizational value beyond his/her team.	Our organization has increased transparency around talent and succession pipelines. Career agility and aspiration is part of our business vernacular and regularly discussed at the executive table.

The employee life-cycle begins from the minute a potential employee is first attracted to the business, flows through the recruitment, onboarding and the career development that follows for each employee through to the exit of the employee from the business and even beyond today, with alumni programs. Influencing the career decisions and needs of each individual as they move within the Career Engagement Grid, and how these initiatives are leveraged by each individual, is part of the employee life-cycle.

As an employee enters, develops and grows in your organization they will be at different stages of the cycle. This impacts their career wants and needs, the value they add, and the value they wish to receive from their organization. The employee life-stage impacts how quickly the individual can activate each piece of the grid and their personal needs within the generic concepts.

Influences on the employee life-cycle

The influences on the employee life-cycle are as follows:

- **Career stage**: This dimension identifies your current career stage, which is not necessarily time related. It moves through *early* career stage, to *growth* and *establishment* phases. Those later in life can be at *mastery* or *late stage* career phases. However, note that if you have made a radical career change mid-career you could still be in growth or establishment phases later in life.

- **Role stage**: This describes current role status. Based typically on length of time in current role, and largely time related, role stage can also take into consideration role-learning needs and readiness for additional responsibilities.

- **Organization stage**: This takes into account organization tenure and whether you are at one or more of the following (not necessarily linear) stages of organization tenure — onboarding, graduate program, talent, development, maintenance, succession, offboarding and retirement.

Additional factors that influence how each individual navigates this grid include other career agility metrics such as:

- **Career-life priorities**
  Your bandwidth for additional development and career focus

- **Acceleration drives**
  Your appetite for acceleration activities or need for deceleration support

- **Pathways preferences**
  Expert vs Leader, experiential requirements

- **Personal mobility**

These influences need to be taken into account when creating organization wide and individually customized career experiences. They allow flexibility for the model to support the unique variety of employees represented.

For example: Let's view how one of the grids is experienced by two different employees based on their employee life-cycle stages.

4 C's	3 E's		
	Individual empowerment:	How Sam is activating his career	How Julia is activating her career
Capability	I bring my best "game" to work — leveraging my motivated talents and building new capability each day, starting from my current role. I am aware of, and ready to step into, stretch opportunities and new roles that fit my own career goals as well as fulfilling organizational need.	Sam is at *mastery* career stage — an experienced performer in his field with in-depth expertise. He is an active mentor, leveraging his talents to support those following in his footsteps. He sees this as a new challenge and an opportunity to build a legacy in his organization.	Julia is mid-career and an active contributor in her role. She is excited about an opportunity to work on a critical business project, showcasing her skill in this area, and taking on the challenge of being the project lead, which is an exciting step up for her.

As you can see, the principle of individual empowerment and building capability remains the same, but how each individual activates this differs depending on their personal employee life-cycle factors.

THE 3 E'S IN MORE DETAIL

Individual empowerment

Let's dive a bit deeper into how the three levels of career engagement play out in an organization and for an individual, manager and business. First, we shall discuss individual empowerment.

Passion + Purpose + Contribution = Commitment

Every day, in every organization and for every person, there is an opportunity for a career connection. From our work with thousands of individual contributors and leaders, we know that there is no single point where career development starts and finishes. In your organization right now, you have people who are eager to add more value, demonstrate capability and step up. You also are likely to have some people who are waiting for you to help them to do this. Enabling people to leverage their passion, fulfill their purpose and convert this to valued contribution creates commitment — for the individual as well as for their manager and organization.

Enabling people to leverage their passion, fulfill their purpose and convert this to valued contribution creates commitment — for the individual as well as for their manager and organization.

A critical element of a career engagement initiative is empowering individuals to bring their passion and purpose to work every day, and to use this understanding to make good career decisions. One of the key messages we impart is that individuals hold the power in career management.

Your organization might be the vehicle for your career, but you need to be in the driving seat!

This message demonstrates how supportive and forceful the organization can be in determining the speed and parameters of career growth: is the organization a sports car or sedan in creating career success moments? Regardless, the individual ultimately determines how much of this is activated. Employees can sit in the driving seat and have the handbrake on firmly, plan and be directive, or can see where the road takes them. The choice is theirs. The key message is that individuals are the leaders of their own careers; critical career decisions and plans should be firmly held in their own hands. Managers and the organization are of course instrumental in creating an environment where career engagement can occur, but ultimately the only person who is responsible for your career is you.

 Empowering your people to make career choices that are right for them, and to understand how to initiate and identify when career success moments are happening, are core parts of a career engagement model.

Building a career competency mindset in each person supports them to make good decisions. Your program should build a workforce that is enabled to demonstrate the following in their career every day:

- **Career alignment**: Bringing your best self to work through understanding key career drivers and living these every day in your current role.

- **Career management**: Aligning career choices to career drivers and current career agility, while actively growing skills and experiences that are critical to personal and organizational success.

- **Strategic career thinking** (for acceleration-minded individuals): Having a clear career vision and a road map of key competency development and experiences needed to reach this goal.

CARLOS: INDIVIDUAL IN THE DRIVING SEAT

Consider Carlos who is driven by the motivator expertise.

Carlos feels most fulfilled when he is able to demonstrate his capability and skill level in his field of project management. He enjoys being called on to support less experienced project managers, and he has played a mentoring role to several "up-and-comers" over the last decade. He has daily satisfaction from applying his skill-set to complex projects that leverage the knowledge and experience he has built during his 20-year career.

Carlos has had opportunities to move into management several times (he is well liked and a great performer), but each time he has evaluated his key career drivers and overall career vision, and decided to continue on his expert pathway. To us, Carlos is demonstrating the career competencies required to make smart decisions for him and his organization.

- **Career forecasting/being a career futurist**: Understanding personal, role, organization and industry changes and including them in career planning to ensure career marketability for the future.

The career choice to move from an expert role to a manager role is a critical career step, and is a common derailer for individuals. Should Carlos have decided to move into a manager role, it is likely that he would have continued to hold a need to work on expert-based projects as an individual contributor. This would have limited his ability to manage his team, or created a feeling of dissatisfaction when he had to hand on those projects to his fellow team members.

Fortunately, Carlos's organization has an expert career path that holds status, recognition and remuneration benefits, so Carlos was able to make a choice that grew his reputation and brand with the organization without compromising his personal career satisfaction. Should Carlos have followed that leadership path, it is likely that his dissatisfaction would have been evident in his performance and productivity — ultimately creating issues for him and his organization.

Carlos's organizational vehicle is one that supports him to align his career choices to his personal vision and drivers, while also supporting business success. His passion, purpose and contribution are aligned to his role right now, and this in turn is evident in his commitment to the organization. Carlos, due to his great performance, and up to date skill-set, is also seen as a critical expert talent by the organization. The executive team can see the value Carlos adds, and it is equally committed to creating ongoing career success and satisfaction for him.

For Carlos to reach this maturity across his career competencies, his organization has empowered him in the following ways:

Career alignment

 Bringing your best self to work through understanding key career drivers and living these every day in your current role.

Carlos has had the benefit of access to the Fuel50 suite of tools to help him uncover his career drivers:

Carlos was able to reflect on this analysis to evaluate his current role satisfaction and create some personal actions to be more in tune with these at work. In particular, Carlos had often been praised for his mentoring of others, and his leaders were encouraging him to apply for management roles. Although Carlos enjoyed mentoring new project managers, his reflection helped him to understand that the knowledge sharing was the key part of this that was rewarding for him. His willingness to support these individuals didn't translate to a desire to manage them on a daily basis.

The career sweet spot

VALUES · TALENTS · PASSIONS

CARLOS'S BUILDING BLOCKS TO CAREER ALIGNMENT

- Utilized smart tools via an employee facing analysis experience, to understand his passions, values, talents, interests, and career agility.

- Supported to reflect and gain insight from his analysis. In Carlos's case his immediate manager was a great career advocate, asking Carlos career questions to deepen reflection. For other individuals in his organization without such a strong manager, this analysis was self-driven via the Fuel50 portal and supported by organizational and team-led insight debriefs and experiences.

- Carlos reviews his analysis on a quarterly basis to map any shifts in focus areas and remind himself of his "best self" drivers. This reflection is reinforced by regular conversations with his manager, development planning discussions, team-based exercises and a business wide values initiative.

Having a clear career vision and a road map of key competency development and experiences needed to reach this goal.

Creating a clear line of sight to future career growth and opportunity is an impact factor for engagement.[2] Having a clear career vision provides an aspirational destination and a way to sense-check career decisions along the way. When we can see how our current role supports us to reach our bigger goal, we are naturally more motivated in our existing position to perform well and exceed expectations.

CARLOS'S BUILDING BLOCKS TO STRATEGIC CAREER THINKING

- He has clarity on how his current role contributes to the organizational goals and strategy

- Through discussions with his own mentor and leveraging his career analysis, Carlos was able to:

  - Link his personal passion and purpose to organizational purpose and business strategy

  - Identify high pay-off competencies for future career growth through career pathway analysis and talent gap analysis

fuel 50

Note, not everyone will want to think strategically about their career. This is an opt-in competency, particularly suitable for those who wish to accelerate or position themselves for career growth beyond their current level. However, all employees should be adept at career management as a minimum.

Career management

 Aligning career choices to career drivers and current career agility, while actively growing skills and experiences that are critical to personal and organizational success.

Carlos has a targeted career plan as well that helps him to tactically manage his career on a short-term basis. While a career strategy might have a long-term lens (a five-year view), a career plan can be orientated to a 12-month or even 90-day cycle.

For Carlos, identifying his team's need to secure a renewal of their biggest client in the next 18 months, his short-term goals are focused on creating key relationships and visible value within that client. For Carlos this is a personal stretch, as although he enjoys building relationships internally, he has let other client managers take a lead communication role with the client. Typically, Carlos likes to let his work speak for itself, which means some of his added value is unnoticed. For the team to win this renewal, Carlos has to step out of his comfort zone to increase client awareness of the additional discretionary effort that is outside the standard brief, and increase the client stakeholders supporting Carlos's organization.

This supports his long-term vision of becoming an industry expert in his field as it builds his own reputation and shows the caliber of his contribution.

CARLOS'S BUILDING BLOCKS TO CAREER MANAGEMENT

Through Carlos's regular development discussions and his manager's team-planning sessions, he has an:

- Understanding of immediate business need and key team priorities through clear objective-setting with his team and manager

- Understanding where he can add additional value to achieving these goals, above and beyond business-as-usual activity.

Coupled with his vision and strategic gap analysis, Carlos and his manager were to create a short-term career management plan that benefited both the organization and Carlos.

Career forecasting

Understanding personal, role, organization and industry changes and including them in career planning to ensure career marketability for the future.

All of us have to re-calibrate our career plan regularly. Change is constant in today's working environment, and this creates challenges and resulting opportunities. Like the boat below, we can be pulled off course by currents or strong winds. We can also take advantage of new technology, enabling our boat to go faster, and be able to keep up with other boats. By altering our working approach in tiny ways regularly, we avoid the shock of having to take a sharp right turn to avoid a potential collision!

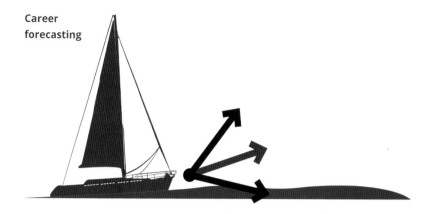

Career forecasting

We can't always predict change, but we can do everything we can to be prepared to change tack if we need to. This is a personal risk management strategy, and a gift you can give your employees to manage their internal and external marketability.

CARLOS'S BUILDING BLOCKS TO BEING A CAREER FUTURIST

- Attending external networking events, conferences or reading industry blogs to understand external thinkers' perspectives on project management and his industry.

- Engaging in future thinking conversations with peers and management on political, environmental, technological and sociological impacts on his role, the team's focus and business success.

- Saying yes to opportunities that build a transferable and broad skill-set and which broaden experiences.

- Building relationships across the organization in different functions to increase personal brand and awareness of alternative future roles and pathways.

This competency is not about encouraging people to leave their current role, but rather helping them to be more valuable in their job right now. It is also about building a more informed and stronger talent bench for business growth and agility in tough times.

Carlos's experience above showcases the impact a powerful manager can have on an individual's career satisfaction. As an organization you can build this competency in your managers over time, while still supporting an individual mindset. Carlos could also have had powerful insight through simple self-analysis, an internal career coach, or peer-led and social learning. Many of our clients start at this point, while they are building manager ability and the skill-set for a Year 2 focus on manager–staff conversations.

THE 3 E'S IN MORE DETAIL: LEADER ENABLEMENT

In the authors' organization, although we live and breathe career engagement in our own offices, team members still bring something new to career conversations. No matter how many years of tenure, each individual is still evolving in their career and life, and their needs are constantly shifting. What this means for Anne and Jo, as leaders, is that even if they think they know team members well, they still need to take the time to listen and understand their career needs in a dedicated session as well as continuing to recognize and create career success moments on a daily basis.

Having meaningful career conversations is a core management competency. If you're not doing this with your people, you are not doing your job properly.

Our clients agree that managers having career conversations is a critical part of their engagement strategy, but they lack the confidence that this will happen or happen well. Building management competency in powerful career conversations and providing enablers to support management agility to respond is often the first step.

For example, after identifying her team had retention and engagement issues, Maria worked closely with Fuel50 and her HR business partner to build her own leadership competency to create a career-engaged team.

On reviewing exit interviews and reflecting on performance conversations, Maria had identified some factors that were hot topics to address:

- The number one reason people were leaving was career development

- Talented staff were exiting to move to other organizations as opposed to moving internally

- People felt blocked or unsure how to activate internal career opportunities and didn't have a clear view of their next step

- People couldn't articulate how their role contributed to organizational goals and success

A quick survey also illustrated that career competency levels across the following four factors were low:

- Career alignment

- Career management

- Strategic career thinking (for acceleration-minded individuals)

- Career forecasting/being a career futurist

Very few of Maria's team were able to articulate their career aspirations in a meaningful way. Maria was also embarrassed to admit that she couldn't articulate what career development meant for each of her staff either. Although her performance reviews included a question about career development needs, people were leaving for opportunities that didn't support their own documented goals. Maria had a clear need to find out more from her people and embed career conversations into her normal management routine, to understand what each person needed from the workplace in order to feel satisfied and successful.

Powerful career conversations

Personal development on career engagement strategies and tactics for career conversations (including a scripted report) built Maria's competency in this space.

Maria was able to leverage her existing coaching skills to take her interactions with staff to a new level. Already a competent and well-liked manager, through career conversations Maria created a greater relationship with each of her staff. Each person was able to articulate what was important to them at work, and this gave Maria insight into simple changes or opportunities that could be facilitated to have a real impact on satisfaction. Each person came away with a greater understanding of the things that were a strong fit for them with their role and organization right now, as well as insight into what they wanted to do more of or change in some way.

For Maria, this is an ongoing part of the way she manages her people and is not seen as a one-off initiative. Each conversation she has with her people becomes richer and deeper, and Maria is able to grow her own skills along the way. The beautiful thing about career conversations is that you don't have to be perfect from day one — just asking simple questions, closing your own mouth and listening will generate a pretty good conversation.

MARIA LAUNCHED HER CAREER PROGRAM TO HER TEAM

- She provided ongoing and unlimited access to smart analysis and planning resources with Fuel50.

- She embedded career conversations into her current management one-on-one interactions, kicking off with a session dedicated to career insight and awareness. Maria committed to the following schedule of formal career interventions:

  - Annual career conversation to facilitate individual understanding of career drivers and support career planning and to support work-shaping activities and changes

  - 10-minute career plan review in each monthly catch-up

  - Quarterly insights and reflection debrief before quarterly team planning and resource allocation.

Maria's role in these conversations is to facilitate insight, support career planning, and raise awareness of how individuals can manage their career, starting from their current role.

- Maria and her HR business partner led a purpose and values session with the team, which helped each person align their individual values and purpose through to organizational purpose and goals and values.

- Maria facilitated an initial group session with her team to kick start career planning and leveraged the self-starter resources available to her via Fuel50.

- On an ongoing and informal basis, Maria was also committed to work towards daily career success moments with her team — recognizing when these occurred and drawing attention to them.

However, we have seen three levels of manager career engagement maturity to which you can aspire:

1 **Current performance contribution**: The ability to coach a staff member to be successful in their current role and team.

2 **Career success contribution**: Supporting the individual to have career success moments across the organization, contributing to other teams and functions.

3 **Future success contribution**: Supporting that individual to fulfill their purpose and passion now and working towards their career vision — regardless of where that might lead them.

These levels are not appropriate for every coaching conversation, but if a team has a typical spread of role stage from entry to maturity, the manager needs to be able to dip in and out of the three levels as required.

Maria, through acting as a career advocate and sounding board, is creating career success moments for each person in her team. She is also building her own management credibility and impact, along with a reputation for accelerating the careers of her team. Maria in turn becomes a magnet for individuals who want to have great careers, attracting talent easily to her team.

Too often we see managers who do everything possible to keep a staff member in their current job and team, despite organizational and individual benefit in moving that person to a different function. Maria demonstrates her capability in the following examples of how she is enabling her staff members to succeed:

MARIA SUPPORTED HER TEAM'S PERSONAL CAREER SUCCESS

Leveraging her existing coaching skills, Maria was able to support her team's personal career success in a variety of ways.

- **Level 1: Current career contribution.** Suzie, for example, had a strong career value of reputation. As a new member of her team, and fairly early in her career, Suzie and her manager Maria are working together to create opportunities for Suzie to build her reputation in her current role. This may be taking a lead on some projects, gaining confidence in speaking up and getting noticed in meetings, or Suzie might have the opportunity to handle some more difficult tasks to build her credibility. These reputation boosters create value for the organization as well as creating career success moments for Suzie.

- **Level 2: Career success contribution.** Anand is also driven by reputation. However, as someone who has been at an establishment level of his career for some time, he is looking for more stretch. Maria is supporting him to contribute to cross-functional projects in areas where he can showcase his capability to a wider audience. This has the advantage of providing additional challenge for Anand, while adding value outside of his immediate team. This will likely retain Anand in Maria's team a bit longer as he completes these projects, but it will also prepare him for future moves in that organization.

- **Level 3: Future success contribution:** Jacqueline also highly values reputation. She has established a strong reputation in her business, but she is seeking to contribute more strategically to her industry. Representing her company at conferences or industry events is an exciting proposition, so Maria and Jacqueline have actively pitched Jacqueline to the internal communications team as a potential speaker at these events. In the meantime, she has continued to speak at internal events and local networking groups to further grow her reputation as a great speaker. These events in no way take away from Jacqueline's daily role, and in fact they enhance her performance as she constantly seeks to live the best-practice models she espouses.

Managers don't own their employees — you are only borrowing them for a short period of time. You must return the employee to the broader organization with "interest." When they leave you, they must do so more skilled, more engaged and adding more value than when they joined.

A leader who is recognized as a talent magnet and "career builder" often becomes highly visible to employees. People are keen to join these leaders, because they see the visible career success stories that eventuate, as people progress to better opportunities. As we operate now in a highly connected social world, the career visibility and support that you create when you operate as a talent magnet and career contributor can also significantly enhance your own personal career success.

THE 3 E'S IN MORE DETAIL:

Organizational effectiveness

Most of the clients we work with who have a business imperative to increase engagement, reduce attrition or manage succession are tasked with this over a three-year period. That timing feels about right — it is enough time to have some real traction, but short enough that the business sees results when they need them. This not only gives time for you to educate your workforce about what career engagement means, but you can build business appetite and leader competency, creating a model that becomes embedded in business-as-usual activity. Career engagement becomes the way we lead and manage our people, the way our people drive their own success and happiness, and the way we plan for succession, and as a result of this embeddedness in the way things are done, it is not one of those HR initiatives that tires and is forgotten.

While carrots and sticks worked successfully in the twentieth century, that's precisely the wrong way to motivate people for today's challenges.[3]

We talked about career engagement as a symphony, with multiple career engagement instruments working together to create an engaged workforce. We have detailed some key parts in our orchestra already — the individual empowerment section and the manager enablement section. The organization has its own critical role to play in building momentum and synergy, with the whole orchestra conducted by the CEO or board.

Having the sponsorship of the executive team is a significant contributor to a successful career engagement project.

HR is often the internal project owner of organization-led initiatives, and it is responsible for release of supporting tools and manager development. We have highlighted how two levels of the career engagement model work at an individual level and a management level. At an organization level, we recommend a career engagement focus to be embedded as follows:

- Onboarding — continuing the career promise articulated in recruitment by supporting new recruits to see how they can build a motivating career path with your organization starting with their current role. Some organizations even begin this pre-hire.

- Staff retention programs — providing enablers to management to support work shaping and career customizations, unique to each individual.

- Graduate programs — building key career competencies that support ongoing performance and success, following the intensive attention of a graduate initiative.

- Engagement — identifying key engagement metrics related to career that the organization wants to shift, and dedicating resource and attention to them.

- Diversity initiatives — creating customized career pathways and targeted career growth programs for target demographic groups within the organization.

- High potential programs — matching individual aspirations and career/agility drivers to accelerate learning opportunities, ensuring increased program completion and personal and business benefit.

- Succession planning — understanding potential successors' career aspirations to ensure alignment with business expectations.

- Learning development — facilitating unique development programs and opportunities that build experiences and talents that support individual career goals and organizational bench strength.

- Career pathways development — taking an innovative look at career pathways to support a talent-actualized workforce with the talent strength to move the organization forward, and increasing personal success and satisfaction.

 Career development needs to be a working component of the overall talent management strategy and plan.

— MARY ANN BOPP[4]

NOTES

1 Crawley, M. and Fulton, A. *Global Career Management Best Practices Research Report*. In Press (2014).

2 See Aon Hewitt (2014). *Trends in Global Employee Engagement Report.* Retrieved from: www.aon.com/attachments/human-capital-consulting/2014-trends-in-global-employee-engagement-report.pdf; Gallup Institute (2013). *State of the American Workplace: Employee engagement insights for US business leaders*. Retrieved from: www.gallup.com/strategicconsulting/163007/state-american-workplace.aspx; Haygroup (2014a). *Preparing for Take-off*. Retrieved from: http://atrium.haygroup.com/downloads/marketingps/ww/Preparing%20for%20take%20off%20-%20 executive%20summary.pdf.

3 Pink, D.H. (2011). *Drive: The Surprising Truth About What Motivates Us*. Penguin, New York, NY.

4 Bopp, M.A., Bing, D. and Forte-Trammell, S. (2009). *Agile Career Development: Lessons and Approaches from IBM*. Pearson Education, Boston, Massachusetts.

10 Organization Best Practices for Transformational Career Engagement

Activating the four foundational pillars and the three levels of career engagement.

ACTIVATING CAREER ENGAGEMENT

Our clients are seeking to increase career empowerment, helping individual staff members navigate the world of work, while supporting their line managers to have regular career conversations. We find that this is often a real passion for our internal client sponsor, but one that they find difficult to tackle. They know there is a valid business case, as detailed in Chapter 3 of this book and validated by our own best-practice benchmark survey. However, our clients are often stumped as to how to break this down into a simple, scalable and easily justifiable (in terms of return on investment) initiative.

For organizations we work with, the following illustrates pain points which have been tackled through a career engagement strategy:

ISSUES RESOLVED WITH A CAREER ENGAGEMENT STRATEGY

- Recent increase in employee turnover and approaches to staff from external organisations

- Regulatory requirements to report on diversity statistics and executive directives to increase representation of target demographics

- An aging workforce with succession risks

- Low engagement in key demographics, such as 25–29 year olds or 30–40 year olds

- Low development "engagement ratings" despite the fact that more than 60% of roles have been filled internally

- Need to retain talent and expertise in older workers

- Need to create understanding of organizational values and purpose and help people understand the role they have in bringing this to life

This chapter presents practical ways to tackle the above, and how to activate the 4 C's and 3 E's across the employee life-cycle. It also highlights some core hygiene factors that need to be in place along the way.

Please note the following examples are not designed to be prescriptive. Instead, pick a point that makes sense for your organization's career engagement maturity and create a long-term approach with review and adaptations along the way. Building layers of initiative over time is the approach often chosen by our organizations as they educate, socialize and build leader and individual competency in career management.

Your organizational needs will also shift, so agility in how you approach career engagement is needed to make sure messaging stays relevant and meaningful.

SCOPE, MESSAGING AND TACTICS

An optimal initiative will likely include the following messages and tactics. Each area is critical to the overall impact in career engagement.

Organizational enablement/effectiveness

 Supporting activation of the four pillars — capability, compatibility, contribution and communication.

Scope:

- Career engagement framework is scalable and sustainable across geography, time and employee level.
- Career engagement is established as a critical People/Human Resources portfolio.
- Career engagement is seen as a foundational strategy for talent and employee engagement.
- The overarching strategy is inclusive, strategic, visible and impactful (outcomes focused).

Messaging:

- Career engagement is sponsored by the CEO/executive team and is owned by a senior HR professional.
- Career engagement is a long-term business strategy and not simply a time-based initiative.

- Career engagement impacts our business profitability and individual satisfaction, and is critical to our business and our people's success.

Tactics:

- Multiple career engagement advocates and experts are developed across the business.

- Internal sponsorship is evident — in particular at executive level — from leaders and managers enacting the strategy.

- A three-year layered approach is developed and committed to with regular return on investment review.

- Critical stakeholders and advocates across the organization are regularly upskilled and engaged in new strategy development and roll-out.

- Initiatives are not developed in isolation but support broader business and HR strategy:

    - Initiative communications and activities support a compelling employer brand and are consistent with other messages

    - Initiatives support existing talent and high potential programs, providing additional insight into talent aspirations and development needs

    - Initiatives support organizational agility through building a more agile workforce with diversity tactics, work shaping and lattice pathway management.

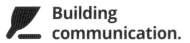

Building communication.

Scope:

- All emerging and existing leaders within the organization including influencers, mentors and coaches who may not have direct reports.

Messaging:

- Creating career engagement teams is a core management competency that is essential to success in our organization.

- At a minimum, leaders will have one meaningful career conversation with each team member per annum — great leaders will do more.

- A successful leader is one who builds diverse talent for our organization, advocating for this talent beyond their current team, supporting business needs for critical competency growth and talent management.

- Great leaders facilitate work shaping and individualized career development growth and pathways, creating a diverse and engaged workforce.

Tactics:

- Each employee has a customized career proposition built in conjunction with their manager, over successive career conversations. These career conversations occur in line with organizational rhythms such as development planning sessions, team planning sessions, individual goal-setting, and in line with individual employee life-cycle events or challenges.

    - Leaders have ongoing support, training and development in how to continue to grow competency in career engaging behaviors.

- Senior and executive leaders model this behavior with their own direct reports.

- Managers are empowered to negotiate flexible work and other work-shaping arrangements with their direct reports.

- Forums are developed where leaders can advocate for talent across business silos, and specific lattice opportunities for individuals are discussed.

- Leaders who build diverse career-engaged teams and add to the organizational talent bank are recognized and rewarded.

Individual empowerment/engagement

 ## Building capability, compatibility and contribution.

Scope:

- Organization wide reach — delivering a career proposition to every person, regardless of role, location and hours.

- Targeted sub-programs that support specific groups (e.g. high potential) within the wider employee footprint.

- Delivered across the entire employee life-cycle from entry to exit.

Messaging:

- Career management as a partnership between employer and employee, but driven and owned by the employee.

- Initiative challenges positional and hierarchical-based career fixation and instead encourages individuals to explore competency or experience-based career planning and a lattice mindset.

- Focus on agility — build individual and organizational agility through experiential career growth and development of competency depth.

- Individual compatibility (values and purpose alignment) to organizational goals is important and reflection on how you can bring your best self to work is encouraged.

Tactics:

- Each employee empowered with career insight and discovery tools to articulate current compatibility and capability and supported to map a custom career path. This is available to each employee as and when they wish to activate it.

- Regular meaningful career conversations between employer and employee are mandated, so each individual is guaranteed at least one career coaching conversation per annum.

- Opportunities to engage in non-business as usual activities such as cross-silo projects, mentoring, coaching and networking is supported by organizational process and communications.

- Individuals can access information about personal career engagement tactics though a variety of easily accessible methods, such as webinars, e-learning and workshops, and are encouraged to do so by their leader.

We recommend you complete our Career Engagement Benchmark survey to reflect on which practices are currently in place and which areas would be appropriate for your initiative to tackle.[1]

BEST PRACTICE IN ACTION: CORPORATE EXAMPLE

Let's now look at how this is rolled out in terms of a sample organizational initiative. The following outlines our best-practice career engagement model for a sample individual (Suzie), manager (Lee) and organization (Ascendant Ltd). Note you might not have all of these organizational initiatives; we have simply included ones common to our clients to illustrate how a career engagement initiative is embedded in people initiatives.

> **Career engagement is a continual process — it isn't completed with a one-off project but is an ongoing strategic business focus, embedded into business-as-usual activity**

ASCENDANT LTD CAREER ENGAGEMENT CHALLENGE

Ascendant Ltd are in a market where their real competitive advantage is people. The capacity to provide skilled, reputable and expedient delivery also sets apart Ascendant Ltd from several competitors. However, Ascendant Ltd is challenged in that their population of talent is aging, and while the tenure of their senior "masters" is long and retention high, the "up and coming" generation of professionals has a high degree of employee churn and general dissatisfaction.

While Ascendant Ltd has several years of secured work ahead through long-term government contracts, there is a high succession risk over the next two to five years as the masters move into retirement age. The pool of potential talent for mid-level professionals is also limited, with an additional challenge of unique requirements specific to Ascendant Ltd's area of specialization.

Engagement scores show a level of career disengagement.

Ascendant Ltd's approach

Ascendant Ltd targeted *career engaged* as a key driver of overall engagement and business success. As career engagement is a critical competitive advantage, retaining and building talent is a strategic priority. Read further to understand the initiatives Ascendant Ltd introduced and the map these have to the 4 C's and the 3 E's.

This program was led by Alana, the Chief People Officer, as a strategic three-year initiative. She approached this as a culture change program, leveraging technology and learning and development tactics to create an impact on engagement scores. Socialization, communication and stakeholder management, as with any change initiative, were critical to Alana's success, and even with CEO sponsorship, Alana had to put in place strategies to ensure understanding and buy-in across the business.

A key metric for Alana was increasing overall engagement scores of existing staff, with particular focus on movement of the career development questions. Alana approached this across three key areas:

- Building individual career ownership and career insight

- Growing manager competency in career engagement

- Championing organizational processes and initiatives that allowed work shaping, lattice career movement and individual career actualization.

Critical components in her strategy are detailed below:

- **Onboarding**: Ascendant Ltd build personal awareness of values and career drivers into the employee career experience from day one. As part of the onboarding experience, the scene is set for ongoing career conversations with management and the opportunity to create a unique career journey with the organization.

- **Career boot camps**: Opportunities to grow career clarity are offered through group career boot camps, webinars and e-learning. Individuals can opt in to programs that help them to understand career drivers, talents and interests and set career goals. These are outside of standard team–manager conversations, but they support each individual to see their future career pathway with Ascendant Ltd and take these goals to their manager for support.

- **Career touch-point**: As part of standard manager–team member conversations and development discussions, a focus is held on how each person can add value to organizational goals. A clear link is made between individual drivers and current job fit, supporting each person to add value through their unique combination of talents, motivators and values. Development planning supports that individual to reach broader career goals, while supporting their team to achieve business objectives.

- **Career decision making**: As part of applications for development spend, new roles or promotions, individuals submit a career plan. This encourages each person to set their own career goals before making critical career decisions.

- **Expert and leader pathways**: In addition to leadership pathways, Ascendant Ltd has also created high status expert roles that allow individuals to grow in seniority and salary along a professional pathway without taking on significant management responsibility. This will counter the bottleneck of experts at mid level and encourage further personal stretch and business impact.

- **Career leadership development**: Career engagement is seen as a critical management skill and is reviewed annually. Each leader is accredited as a qualified Career Engagement Leader and is able to support diverse work groups to reach individual career aspirations while maintaining organizational goals. An 18-month program of career leadership development is mandatory for each leader and includes one-on-one personal career strategy guidance (each leader has a great career experience!), e-learning, group mentorship and team feedback.

- **Customized working experiences**: Managers are supported to create customized working experiences for each team member. With a plethora of team-tailored options within each manager's control, managers can create a better working fit for each person. Options are specific to each team's particular needs, but they include opportunities to accept or recommend short-term role transfers, project rotations for employees, flexible hours/shifts, team leadership rotations, meeting facilitation practice, mentorships, skill-based pay and more. Managers are encouraged to suggest new ideas for career engagement tactics to the organization monthly or more regularly.

- **Career analysis tools and resources**: People leaders are provided with career factor analysis and planning tools to support easy but meaningful career conversations with people. Team workshop guides, individual coaching program script and analytic tools and automated reports provide the resources each leader needs to create a career engagement program, specific to their team's needs.

- **Graduate program**: Ascendant Ltd's graduate program provides new graduates with the opportunity to experience various areas of business. A Career Jumpstart program helps each graduate set a personal career goal for their 18-month program, ensuring they are leveraging the opportunity to the best of their ability. Career capital building concepts such as networking, personal brand and reputation management help each person to shine during the initiative.

- **Talent program**: Ascendant Ltd's talent program incorporates aspiration-setting as well as the standard performance and potential matrix. This helps each person opt in to the program based on aspirational fit, ensuring that the targeted talent program is well matched to that individual's goals. This ensures better program retention and completion, maximizing the return of both individual and organizational investment. Career factor analytics also paint a clear picture of any organization risks or strengths of the talent population including career and role stage spread, acceleration needs and talent matrix.

- **Talent forum:** A talent forum allows leaders across Ascendant Ltd to share up and coming talent profiles and discuss cross-silo projects, alternate mentors and talent moves. Line level managers are tasked with providing quarterly talent reports to their functional heads, which are then discussed at this senior level.

How Ascendant Ltd's career engagement strategy was experienced by employee, Suzie.

SUZIE

Suzie is a mid-level career professional with eight years' proven track record. She has key career drivers of expertise, reputation and appreciation and is highly motivated by being considered a "guru" in her field. Suzie has aspirations of achieving senior status in her industry, and enjoys working on challenging problems. She was attracted to her current employer by their ability to secure complex government projects and her manager's desire to pull together experts into his project teams. Suzie is looking forward to her new role, but is a bit worried as she has two teenage sons who require a lot of her attention at present.

Suzie's career experience (Year 1)

- **Career stage**: Establishment
- **Role stage**: Entry
- **Organization stage**: Onboarding, Individual Contributor Development

Note: The following is a fluid matrix and activities can often sit in multiple boxes; they are synchronous and not in isolation.

Compatibility	
Individual empowerment	**The onboarding experience:** this helps Suzie to link her personal values to the organization's values: Suzie is able to articulate her personal and career values and how this will support her personal brand at Ascendant Ltd.
Manager enablement	**First 30 days — career factor meeting:** Lee, Suzie's manager, meets with Suzie early in her new role. Establishing career conversations as business as usual. Lee sets the scene for ongoing career goal-setting and transparency. Lee uses this first career factor meeting to uncover Suzie's career drivers and set a 90-day plan for career success.
Manager enablement	**Group data:** Suzie completes her online career factor assessments. Suzie's feedback on values adds to the organizational insight into employee beliefs. These analytics are added to the overall groups and are used to support a new reward and recognition program specific to Suzie's business unit.

Capability	
Individual empowerment	**Career boot camps:** Suzie has indicated she has high life demands at the moment. This has meant that while she has been committed to high performance, she has been unable to opt in to after-work development. Lee has supported Suzie to find lunchtime learning sessions and also created (in standard work hours) team activities to support broader team cohesiveness without disadvantaging Suzie. Suzie and Lee have also agreed that the 12-month focus is performance and not stretch, though this might change once Suzie has more "bandwidth" to devote to extra learning.
Manager enablement	**Quarterly career catch-ups:** The first 12 months of Suzie's tenure is characterized by opportunities for Suzie to prove herself to her colleagues and clients. Starting Suzie with less critical projects, Lee was able to build Suzie's competency in a new environment, while giving her enough "wins" for Suzie to have a sense of expertise and career achievement.
Manager enablement	**Organizational performance:** Suzie's desire to perform at a high level contributes to several successful projects and client references. Although Suzie is working on minor projects, these are highly profitable and considered key to organizational success.

Contribution	
Individual empowerment	**Career boot camps:** Suzie takes advantage of the lunchtime career sessions facilitated by an internal career champion. Suzie brainstorms a career vision and creates a clear blueprint of what she personally wants to achieve in her first 12 months. A key focus is building a reputation for performance.
Manager enablement	**Quarterly career catch-ups:** Suzie brings insights from her boot camp sessions to her conversations with Lee. Excited about her career vision and with clarity about what she wants to achieve, Suzie and Lee had an enjoyable career conversation creating realistic ways for Suzie to add more value to projects and excel.
Manager enablement	**Organizational performance:** The organization has retained Suzie after that critical 90-day retention risk period. She is motivated and positive.

Communication	
Individual empowerment	**Quarterly career catch-ups/career touch-points:** Suzie has built a transparent and trusting relationship with her leader. As such she feels able to articulate some work-shaping needs that would support greater personal engagement.
Manager enablement	**Organizational career engagers:** Suzie's manager is supported in his request to provide variant working scenarios for his team. Although Suzie prefers a 9 to 5 work schedule, she is able to change her schedule as needed to fit in school concerts and work a Saturday morning instead of Thursday afternoon to gain some personal alone time (a gift in a household with two almost grown sons!).
Manager enablement	**Organizational performance:** By enabling leaders with work-shaping tactics, the organization builds loyalty from Suzie and creates a strong advocate — she is often talking about her great workplace with friends, family and colleagues, reinforcing the strong external and internal EVP of which Ascendant Ltd is proud.

For Suzie, Year 1 has been all about building capability and reputation. She has been given the opportunity to shine early in her tenure, while remaining highly supported in her role. Although her home life is very demanding, Suzie has been given the flexibility she needs to achieve the balance she seeks.

Let's see how Suzie is tracking two years later.

Suzie's career experience (Year 3)

- **Career stage**: Establishment
- **Role stage**: Contributor
- **Organization stage**: Mentoring, Succession

Note: The following is a fluid matrix and activities can often sit in multiple boxes; they are synchronous and not in isolation.

Compatibility	
Individual empowerment	The last two years have confirmed Suzie's desire for an ongoing expertise pathway. Although Suzie has been presented with management opportunities (Lee has since moved laterally to another area of the organization), she has been able to make an informed decision about what will bring her career satisfaction and success.
Manager enablement	**Quarterly career catch-ups:** Ongoing catch-ups with her new manager Maria have maintained Suzie's personal career engagement and ongoing career development and support.
Manager enablement	**Group data:** Like Suzie, all employees at Ascendant Ltd regularly update their Fuel50 profile. As a result, over the last three years the organization has created a record of key employee drivers, talent strengths, development areas and agility needs. In particular, the career stage data of talents provided insight into a concerning weighting of mastery and entry stages. This has led to a significant recruitment and talent drive for mid-level professionals. Suzie is an example of the success of that program.

Capability	
Individual empowerment	**Internal mentor:** Suzie is feeling ready to take on more stretch and development. She has activated an internal mentorship that has allowed her to access the advocacy and advice of a senior specialist in the organization. This mentor has already provided Suzie with insight into an upcoming project team and recommended her to the project sponsor as a valuable contributor.
Manager enablement	**Talent program:** Suzie was invited to the Ascendant Ltd talent program in January, but after discussion with the talent manager and her mentor, she will be placed in the pool for the following year instead. This ties in nicely with Suzie's youngest son going to university and it is when Suzie will be ready to commit to the late nights and additional study required. In addition, this gives Suzie another 12 months to take on some stretch projects to build her competency depth further, which she believes will support her to better manage the talent program demands.
Manager enablement	**Talent program:** Through Suzie's ownership and understanding of her career agility and current needs, the talent manager was able to avoid a possible derailing person in the talent group who would have tied up valuable resources. Suzie's well thought out decision allowed the talent group to involve another staff member who can activate the opportunity right now, and kept Suzie, a talented staff member, retained in her current role.

Contribution	
Individual empowerment	Suzie has moved to a contributor level in her team. With two years' tenure under her belt, she has built solid team and client relationships, providing confidence to her existing and new clients.
Manager enablement	**Quarterly career catch-ups/career touch-points:** These ongoing catch-ups support Suzie and her manager to plan for Suzie's move into a mastery stage, and also to ensure there is sufficient challenge in Suzie's role right now. Suzie and Maria are also looking at ways to take Suzie's experience and expertise into other business areas, perhaps through a short secondment, which would deepen her own competencies but also bring different perspectives to another team.
Manager enablement	**Business performance:** The early investment in Suzie as she joined the team and came up to speed is clearly returning great value through the retention of her talents. This is part of a broader strategy of building a foundation of talent for future e-business need.

Communication	
Individual empowerment	**Quarterly career catch-ups/career touch-points:** Suzie continues to feel supported to discuss her changing career needs. Although her values and purpose are largely unchanged, how Suzie wants to activate these has shifted.
Manager enablement	**Quarterly career catch-ups/career touch-points:** An organization wide approach to career engagement meant that when Suzie had a change in manager, her new manager was skilled in continued career conversations. This eased the transition for Suzie, as the new manager quickly held one-on-one career conversations with each staff member to understand the career drivers and aspirations of her new team.
Manager enablement	**Talent forum:** At a senior level, Suzie's talent profile (which she created) is shared and discussed. The senior talent team take ownership of ensuring that they support Suzie as much as possible to activate her career goals.

For Suzie, the past few years have been a personal career highlight. Despite management changes, she has continued to feel supported in her career and personal goals and has been able to maintain a balance that works for her. She has been able to add significant business value through her project contribution and has been recognized through an invitation to the talent program. Despite not feeling ready for this, Suzie continues to grow and stretch with the support of her mentor and is able to put herself back in the talent pool for consideration next year. This is a great example of transparency and alignment.

How this approach was experienced by Suzie's manager, Lee.

LEE

Lee was a project expert promoted internally to a management role. He was a highly competent performer but found that he enjoyed the management and resource allocation side of projects, and he liked to leverage other individuals' expertise to reach business goals. A management role has been a good fit for Lee, and he enjoys supporting his team to great success. However, before this career engagement initiative, Lee was frustrated by a high employee turnover in his team. His style of management had been very much "painting within the lines" and relatively inflexible. Lee also had a one-style-fits-all approach to reward and recognition, and had limited time for individual catch-ups.

The Career Engagement Leadership program and supporting organizational frameworks has helped Lee as follows:

- They have reinforced the importance of one-on-one career conversations with each staff member and enable Lee to prioritize them.

- Individual empowerment programs have educated his team while he was growing his own leadership competency. Although initial career conversations were relatively transactional, Lee has been able to deepen them as he has grown in competency and his team has become more comfortable with these concepts.

- Lee has been successful in customizing his engagement approach to each person. Now that he has a repertoire of career engagement tactics, each of his team has a tailored working proposition that suits them — this is work shaping in action.

- They have encouraged an approach that supports greater team diversity. Lee is more open to individuals with different life goals and needs, and he sees this diversity as reducing team risk and silo thinking.

- Lee has been inspired and mentored by his own manager, who has helped Lee target his own career development and think more laterally about how he builds career competency and business reputation.

By building such a strong career-engaged team, Lee has built his own value to the organization and was offered a high profile team to manage and retain.

We have viewed a working case study of how the 4 C's and 3 E's can play out in a typical organization. However, we present some final notes on the hygiene factors of best practice. These elements also evolve within an engagement project, so even if some of these factors are not present, your initiative will have the effect of building them over time.

Trust

There has to be trust between the employer and employee. Sometimes this trust is reminiscent of the trust in and expectations for their children that parents have; guilt can go a long way towards keeping us in line, far more so than a raft of compliance and clock-in measures that are designed to make sure you arrive and leave on time. The "stick" style of workplace should have gone out with the industrial era, as it does nothing but foster a disengaged, resentful and reactionary workforce. On the other hand, high expectation delivered through trust is far more likely to deliver high performance. If you think back to your high school days, you may find that those teachers that got the best from you were those who had the highest expectations of you.

Trust comes into play in your career engagement initiative because transparency of conversation, manager career advocacy and ongoing activation of career aspirations build this incrementally. The more conversations you have with your leader about your career, where you come away motivated and supported, the more open you will be the next time. Even a very transactional career conversation — where intentions are good on both sides — will add to a feeling of trust and engagement.

Alignment

Where there is alignment of goals, missions and objectives between the individual and the organization you are creating the foundation for high performance and high engagement. This alignment is a key to allowing people the work freedom to bring their best selves to work. Several tactics in your career engagement strategy can deliver this: personal awareness and insight, manager conversations, and group purpose-based workshops or webinars can highlight and advance this feeling of alignment.

Inclusiveness

The best career engagement initiatives we have seen are inclusive from two points of view. Firstly, they include the whole of business. This is not just about talent, your high potentials and your succession risks. To deliver the engagement and productivity benefits, it has to be whole of business, so that every employee has an opportunity to contribute to the best of their abilities.

Also, the best performing employees will be open to a bottom-up approach to engagement. What we are talking about here is the ability of every employee to align their personal values at work, and use as many of their talents and capabilities as possible at work. This scalability and whole-of-business approach is what will allow you to increase the ratio of engaged to disengaged in your workplace. We all know what it feels like when we are the recipient of those really memorable service moments. Engagement is infectious. Allowing people the chance to be their best at work will allow you to build a culture of engagement. It is that simple with the right tools and processes.

The second aspect to an inclusive workplace is one which supports a diverse workforce. There are real benefits to having an inclusive workforce that embraces all ages, ethnicities and working needs.

Transparency

We haven't touched much on this, so let us take a stand now. Initiatives like this need to be transparent, widely communicated and discussed from the top table through to the recruitment line. Too often we hear about high potential programs or succession strategies that are "hidden" from the broader population and sometimes even the talent themselves. To build a trust-based workplace, transparency is key. Education of leaders and employees helps to eliminate fears over how to respond to retention risks and to the hard questions around aspiration, work-shaping needs and inclusion on high status programs. Fear of the conversation shouldn't get in the way of transparency.

Executive sponsorship

The best organizations that we work with and those that are winning best places to work awards are those that have executive-level sponsorship and ideally are CEO driven. Increasingly, we are seeing a trend towards career development as being a high priority focus for CEOs, even more so than we are seeing from HR practitioners that would typically be seen as owners of career management. At a recent global HR executive conference there was a high proportion of delegates reporting that CEOs were discussing in their round table forums that talent retention and career development need to be priority areas for the business. Some even have it as an organizational strategic priority, most evident to date in the insurance sector.

CONCLUSION

Remember, this chapter is about a long game — not a short one. Creating a career-engaged workforce occurs over time, as your workforce and leaders grow with the program. It is about incremental changes for each individual, delivered by agile HR programs and leader enablement, creating an overall engagement strategy. You don't have to eat the elephant all in one go — just choose your fork, and dig in for the first course!

NOTES

1   The Fuel50 *Best In Class Career Benchmark Survey* can be completed via the following link: http://go.fuel50.com/benchs

REFERENCES

Allen, D.G., Shore, L.M. and Griffeth, R.W. (2003). The role of perceived organizational support and supportive human resource practices in the turnover process. *Journal of Management*, 29(1), 99–118.

Allred, K.D. and Smith, T.W. (1989). The hardy personality: Cognitive and physiological responses to evaluative threat. *Journal of Personality and Social Psychology*, 56(2), 257.

Aon (2010). *Aon Consulting Engagement 2.0 Employee Survey* — U.S. Retrieved from: www.aon.com/ready/attachments/engagement_2.pdf.

Aon Hewitt (2011). *Trends in Global Employee Engagement Report*. Retrieved from: www.aon.com/attachments/thought-leadership/Trends_Global_Employee_ Engagement_Final.pdf.

Aon Hewitt (2013). *Trends in Global Employee Engagement Report*. Retrieved from: www.aon.com/attachments/human-capital-consulting/2013_Trends_in_ Global_Employee_Engagement_Report.pdf.

Aon Hewitt (2014). *Trends in Global Employee Engagement Report*. Retrieved from: www.aon.com/attachments/human-capital-consulting/2014-trends-in- global-employee-engagement-report.pdf.

Appelbaum, S.H. and Santiago, V. (1997). Career development in the plateaued organization. *Career Development International*, 2(1), 11–20.

Avolio, B.J., Walumbwa, F.O. and Weber, T.J. (2009). Leadership: Current theories, research, and future directions. *Annual Review of Psychology*, 60, 421–49.

Bakker, A.B. (2010). Engagement and "job crafting": engaged employees create their own great place to work. In S. Albrecht (ed.), *Handbook of Employee Engagement: Perspectives, Issues, Research and Practice*. Edward Elgar, Cheltenham, pp. 229–44.

Bakker, A.B. (2011). An evidence-based model of work engagement. *Current Directions in Psychological Science*, 20(4), 265–69.

Bakker, A.B. and Bal, M.P. (2010). Weekly work engagement and performance: A study among starting teachers. *Journal of Occupational and Organizational Psychology*, 83(1), 189–206.

Bakker, A.B., Demerouti, E. and Sanz-Vergel, A.I. (2014). Burnout and work engagement: The JD-R approach. *Annual Review of Organizational Psychology and Organizational Behavior*, 1, 389–411.

Bandura, A. (*1977*). *Social Learning Theory*. General Learning Press, New York, NY.

BBC Business News Report, January 28, 2014.

Beechler, S. and Woodward, I.C. (2009). The global "war for talent". *Journal of International Management*, 15, 273–85.

Benko, C. and Anderson, M. (2010). *The Corporate Lattice: Achieving High Performance in the Changing World of Work*. Harvard Business Review Press, Boston, Massachusetts.

Benko, C. and Weisberg, A. (2007). *Mass Career Customization: Aligning the Workplace with Today's Nontraditional Workforce*. Harvard Business Review Press, Boston, Massachusetts.

Benko, C., Erickson, R., Hagel, J. and Wong, J. (2014). *Beyond Retention: Build Passion and Purpose*. Deloitte University Press. Retrieved from: http://dupress.com/ articles/hc-trends-2014-beyond-retention/.

Benson, G.S. (2006). Employee development, commitment and intention to turnover: A test of "employability" policies in action. *Human Resource Management Journal*, 16(2), 173–92.

Berg, J.M., Dutton, J.E. and Wrzesniewski, A. (2008). What is job crafting and why does it matter? Retrieved from: http://positiveorgs.bus.umich.edu/wp-content/uploads/What-is-Job-Crafting-and-Why-Does-it-Matter1.pdf.

Berg, J.M., Dutton, J.E. and Wrzesniewski, A. (2013). Job crafting and meaningful work. In B.J. Dik, Z.S. Byrne and M.F. Steger (eds), *Purpose and Meaning in the Workplace*. American Psychological Association, Washington, DC, pp. 81–104.

Bersin by Deloitte (2014). HCI Employee Engagement Conference, 2014.

Bhatnagar, J. (2007). Talent management strategy of employee engagement in Indian ITES employees: Key to retention. *Employee Relations*, 29(6), 640–63.

Blenko, M.W., Mankins, M.C. and Rogers, P. (2010). *Decide & Deliver: 5 Steps to Breakthrough Performance in Your Organization*. Harvard Business School Publishing, Boston, Massachusetts.

Bopp, M., Bing, D. and Forte-Trammell, S. (2007). *Agile Career Development, Lessons and Approaches from IBM*. IBM Press.

Bopp, M.A., Bing, D. and Forte-Trammell, S. (2009). *Agile Career Development: Lessons and Approaches from IBM*. Pearson Education, Boston, Massachusetts.

Bosch, J.A., de Geus, E.J., Carroll, D., Goedhart, A.D., Anane, L.A., van Zanten, J.J.V., . . . and Edwards, K.M. (2009). A general enhancement of autonomic and cortisol responses during social evaluative threat. *Psychosomatic Medicine*, 71(8), 877–85.

Botha, A., Bussin, M. and De Swardt, L. (2011). An employer brand predictive model for talent attraction and retention: original research. *South African Journal of Human Resource Management*, 9(1), 1–12.

Breevaart, K., Bakker, A.B. and Demerouti, E. (2014). Daily self-management and employee work engagement. *Journal of Vocational Behavior*, 84(1), 31–38.

Fuel50 (2013). *Career Agility Trends Research*. Retrieved from: www.fuel50.com/pdf/career-agility-engagement-fuel50-white-paper.pdf.

Chalofsky, N.E. (2010). *Meaningful Workplaces: Reframing How and Where We Work*. John Wiley and Sons, San Francisco.

Chambers, E.G., Foulon, M., Handfield-Jones, H., Hankin, S.M. and Michaels, E.G. (1998). The war for talent. *The McKinsey Quarterly*, 3, 44–57.

Chaufeli, W.B. and Bakker, A.B. (2004). Job demands, job resources, and their relationship with burnout and engagement: A multi-sample study. *Journal of Organizational Behavior*, 25(3), 293–315.

Chen, T.Y., Chang, P.L. and Yeh, C.W. (2004). A study of career needs, career development programs, job satisfaction and the turnover intentions of R&D personnel. *Career Development International*, 9(4), 424–37.

Clark, T. (2012). *The Employee Engagement Mindset: The Six Drivers for Tapping Into the Hidden Potential of Everyone in Your Company*. McGraw-Hill Professional, New York, NY.

Clifton, D.O. and Harter, J.K. (2003). Investing in strengths. In K.S. Cameron, J.E. Dutton and R.E. Quinn (eds), *Positive Organizational Scholarship: Foundations of a New Discipline*. Berrett-Koehler, San Francisco, pp. 111–21.

Corporate Leadership Council (2004). *Driving Performance and Retention through Employee Engagement*. Corporate Executive Board, Washington, DC.

Corporate Leadership Council (2010). *The Role of Employee Engagement on the Return to Growth*. Retrieved from: www.businessweek.com/managing/content/aug2010/ca20100813_586946.htm.

Crawley, M. and Fulton, A. *Global Career Management Best Practices Research Report*. In Press (2014).

Crossley, C.D., Bennett, R.J., Jex, S.M. and Burnfield, J.L. (2007). Development of a global measure of job embeddedness and integration into a traditional model of voluntary turnover. *Journal of Applied Psychology*, 92(4), 1031.

De Vos, A., De Hauw, S. and Van der Heijden, B.I. (2011). Competency development and career success: The mediating role of employability. *Journal of Vocational Behavior*, 79(2), 438–47.

De Vos, A., Dewettinck, K. and Buyens, D. (2008). To move or not to move?: The relationship between career management and preferred career moves. *Employee Relations*, 30(2), 156–75.

Deloitte (2013). *Resetting Horizons; Human Capital Trends 2013*. Retrieved from: www2.deloitte.com/content/dam/Deloitte/global/Documents/ HumanCapital/dttl-hc-hctrendsglobal-8092013.pdf.

Edwards, J.R. (1991). Person–job fit: A conceptual integration, literature review, and methodological critique. In C.L. Cooper and I.T. Robertson (eds), *International Review of Industrial and Organizational Psychology* (vol. 6). John Wiley & Sons, New York, pp. 286–357.

Employee Engagement Report 2011: Blessing White, Inc. Retrieved from: www. slideshare.net/oscartoscano/blessing-white-2011-ee-report.

Employee Engagement ROAD TO SUCCESS, April 2011, JRA. Retrieved from: www. johnrobertson.co.nz/resources.aspx?cat=9.

Fernandes, M. (2012). *Values Based Leadership*. Retrieved from: http://553. membee.com/cms/clients/553/files/Leadership_Program_Nov27.pdf.

Frankl, V.E. (1985). *Man's Search for Meaning*. Simon and Schuster, New York, NY.

Future Work Skills 2020. Retrieved from: www.iftf.org/uploads/media/SR-1382A_ UPRI_future_work_skills_sm.pdf.

Gallup Institute (2013). *State of the American Workplace: Employee engagement insights for US business leaders*. Retrieved from: www.gallup.com/ strategicconsulting/163007/state-american-workplace.aspx.

Gallup Institute (2014). *State of the American Workplace: Employee engagement insights for US business leaders*. Retrieved from: www.gallup.com/ strategicconsulting/163007/state-american-workplace.aspx.

Gecas, V. (1982). The self-concept. *Annual Review of Psychology*, 8, 1–33.

Gerstner, C.R. and Day, D.V. (1997). Meta-analytic review of leader–member exchange theory: Correlates and construct issues. *Journal of Applied Psychology*, 82(6), 827.

Giallonardo, L.M., Wong, C.A. and Iwasiw, C.L. (2010). Authentic leadership of preceptors: Predictor of new graduate nurses' work engagement and job satisfaction. *Journal of Nursing Management*, 18(8), 993–1003.

Glen, C. (2006). Key skills retention and motivation: the war for talent still rages and retention is the high ground. *Industrial and Commercial Training*, 38(1), 37–45.

Grant, A.M. (2007). Relational job design and the motivation to make a prosocial difference. *Academy of Management Review*, 32(2), 393–417.

Groves, K.S. and Feyerherm, A.E. (2011). Leader cultural intelligence in context: Testing the moderating effects of team cultural diversity on leader and team performance. *Group & Organization Management*, 36(5), 535–66.

Hackman, J.R. and Oldham, G.R. (1980). *Work Redesign*. Addison-Wesley, Reading, Massachusetts.

Halbesleben, J. and Wheeler, A. (2008). The relative roles of engagement and embeddedness in predicting job performance and intention to leave. *Work & Stress: An International Journal of Work, Health & Organisations*, 22(3), 242–56.

Halbesleben, J.R.B. (2008). A meta-analysis of work engagement: Relationships with burnout, demands, resources and consequences. In A. Bakker and M.P. Leiter (eds), *Work Engagement: Recent Developments in Theory and Research*. London: Routledge. Retrieved from: www.bls.gov/news.release/pdf/jolts.pdf.

Halbesleben, J.R.B., Osburn, H.K. and Mumford, M.D. (2006). Action research as a burnout intervention: Reducing burnout in the Federal Fire Service. *Journal of Applied Behavioral Science*, 42, 244–66.

Harter, J.K., Schmidt, F.L. and Hayes, T.L. (2002). Business-unit level relationship between employee satisfaction, employee engagement, and business outcomes: A meta-analysis. *Journal of Applied Psychology*, 87, 268–79.

Harter, J.K., Schmidt, F.L., Asplund, J.W., Killham, E.A. and Agrawal, S. (2010). Causal impact of employee work perceptions on the bottom line of organizations. *Perspectives on Psychological Science*, 5(4), 378–89.

HayGroup (2014a). *Preparing for Take-off*. Retrieved from: http://atrium.haygroup.com/downloads/marketingps/ww/Preparing%20for%20take%20off%20-%20executive%20summary.pdf.

HayGroup (2014b). *Global Talent Exodus on the Horizon as Economic Growth Returns*. Retrieved from: www.haygroup.com/ww/press/details.aspx?id=37373.

Hewitt Associates (July 29, 2010). *Percent of Organizations with Falling Engagement Scores Triples in Two Years*. Press release.

Hiller, N., DeChurch, L., Murase, T. and Doty, D. (2011). Searching for leadership outcomes: A 25 year review. *Journal of Management*, 37(4), 1137–77.

Holland, J.L. (1996). Exploring careers with a typology: What we have learned and some new directions. *American Psychologist*, 51(4), 397.

Holland, J.L., Whitney, D.R., Cole, N.S. and Richards, J.M., Jr. (1969). *An Empirical Occupational Classification Derived from a Theory of Personality and Intended for Practice and Research* (ACT Research Report No. 29). American College Testing Program, Iowa City, IA.

Iles, P. (1997). Sustainable high-potential career development: a resource-based view. *Career Development International*, 2(7), 347–53.

Inkson, K. and Arthur, M.B. (2001). How to be a successful career capitalist. *Organizational Dynamics*, 30(1), 48–61.

Inkson, K. and King, Z. (2011). Contested terrain in careers: A psychological contract model. *Human Relations*, 64(1), 37–57.

Judge, T.A. and Piccolo, R.F. (2004). Transformational and transactional leadership: a meta-analytic test of their relative validity. *Journal of Applied Psychology*, 89(5), 755.

Karatepe, O.M., Beirami, E., Bouzari, M. and Safavi, H.P. (2014). Does work engagement mediate the effects of challenge stressors on job outcomes? Evidence from the hotel industry. *International Journal of Hospitality Management*, 36, 14–22.

Kilduff, M., Angelmar, R. and Mehra, A. (2000). Top management-team diversity and firm performance: Examining the role of cognitions. *Organization Science*, 11(1), 21–34.

Knight, D., Pearce, C.L., Smith, K.G., Olian, J.D., Sims, H.P., Smith, K.A. and Flood, P. (1999). Top management team diversity, group process, and strategic consensus. *Strategic Management Journal*, 20(5), 445–65.

Koyuncu, M., Burke, R.J. and Fiksenbaum, L. (2006). Work engagement among women managers and professionals in a Turkish bank: Potential antecedents and consequences. *Equal Opportunities International*, 25, 299–310.

Lazarus, R.S. and Folkman, S. (1984). *Stress, Appraisal, and Coping*. Springer, New York, NY.

Le Blanc, P.M., Hox, J.J., Schaufeli, W.B. and Peeters, M.C.W. (2007). Take care! The evaluation of a team-based burnout intervention program for oncology care providers. *Journal of Applied Psychology*, 92, 213–27.

Luthans, F., Avolio, B.J., Avey, J.B. and Norman, S.M. (2007). Positive psychological capital: Measurement and relationship with performance and satisfaction. *Personnel Psychology*, 60(3), 541–72.

Maguire, H. (2002). Psychological contracts: Are they still relevant? *Career Development International*, 7(3), 167–80.

Maslow, A. (1954). *Motivation and Personality*. Harper, New York, NY.

Meister, J.C. and Willyerd, K. (2010). *The 2020 Workplace: How Innovative Companies Attract, Develop, and Keep Tomorrow's Employees Today*. Harper Business, New York, NY.

Mendes, F. and Stander, M.W. (2011). Positive organization: The role of leader behavior in work engagement and retention. *South African Journal of Industrial Psychology*, 37(1), 1–13.

Minchington, B. (2010). *Employer Brand Leadership: A Global Perspective*, Collective Learning Australia, Torrensville, South Australia.

Mitchell, T.R., Holtom, B.C., Lee, T.W., Sablynski, C.J. and Erez, M. (2001). Why people stay: Using job embeddedness to predict voluntary turnover. *Academy of Management Journal*, 44(6), 1102–21.

NFIB Research Foundation (2014). *The March Report; Uncertainty continues to be the enemy of small businesses*. Retrieved from: www.nfib.com/surveys/small-business-economic-trends/.

Ng, T.W. and Feldman, D.C. (2012). Breaches of past promises, current job alternatives, and promises of future idiosyncratic deals: Three-way interaction effects on organizational commitment. *Human Relations*, 65(11), 1463–86.

Oh, I.S., Guay, R.P., Kim, K., Harold, C.M., Lee, J.H., Heo, C.G. and Shin, K.H. (2014). Fit happens globally: A meta-analytic comparison of the relationships of person–environment fit dimensions with work attitudes and performance across East Asia, Europe, and North America. *Personnel Psychology*, 67(1), 99–152.

Payne, D. (2014) *Kiplingers' Economic Outlooks, March 2014*. Retrieved from: www.kiplinger.com/tool/business/T019-S000-kiplinger-s-economic-outlooks/.

Pink, D.H. (2011). *Drive: The Surprising Truth About What Motivates Us*. Penguin, New York, NY.

Pitt-Catsouphes, M. and Matz-Costa, C. (2008). The multi-generational workforce: Workplace flexibility and engagement. *Community, Work & Family*, 11, 215–29.

Pulse on Leaders (February 19, 2009). Personnel Decisions International, Press release.

Robinson, J. (May 8, 2008). Turning around employee turnover. *The Gallup Business Journal*. Retrieved from: http://businessjournal.gallup.com/content/106912/turning-around-your-turnover-problem.aspx#3.

Rohleder, N., Beulen, S.E., Chen, E., Wolf, J.M. and Kirschbaum, C. (2007). Stress on the dance floor: the cortisol stress response to social-evaluative threat in competitive ballroom dancers. *Personality and Social Psychology Bulletin*, 33(1), 69–84.

Rosso, B.D., Dekas, K.H. and Wrzesniewski, A. (2010). On the meaning of work: A theoretical integration and review. *Research in Organizational Behavior*, 30, 91–127.

Saks, A.M. (2006). Antecedents and consequences of employee engagement. *Journal of Managerial Psychology*, 27, 600–19.

Salanova, M., Schaufeli, W.B., Xanthopoulou, D. and Bakker, A.B. (2010). The gain spiral of resources and work engagement: Sustaining a positive worklife. In A.B. Bakker and M.P. Leiter (eds), *Work Engagement: A Handbook of Essential Theory and Research*. Psychology Press, New York, NY. pp. 118–31.

Schaufeli, W.B. and Bakker, A.B. (2004a). *Talentkeepers Global Talent and Retention Report 2013*. Retrieved from: www.talentkeepers.com/download/2013-TalentKeepers-Employee-Engagement-Retention-Trends-Report-Final.pdf.

Schaufeli, W.B. and Bakker, A.B. (2004b). Job demands, job resources, and their relationship with burnout and engagement: A multi-sample study. *Journal of Organizational Behavior*, 25(3), 293–315.

Schaufeli, W.B. and Bakker, A.B. (2010). Defining and measuring work engagement: Bringing clarity to the concept. *Work Engagement: A Handbook of Essential Theory and Research*. Psychology Press, New York, NY, pp. 10–24.

Semler, R. (1993). *Maverick!: The Success Story Behind the World's Most Unusual Workplace*. Warner Books, New York, NY.

Sin, H.P., Nahrgang, J.D. and Morgeson, F.P. (2009). Understanding why they don't see eye to eye: An examination of leader–member exchange (LMX) agreement. *Journal of Applied Psychology*, 94(4), 1048.

Society of Human Resource Management (2012a). *Jobs Outlook Survey Report: Q4 2012*. Retrieved from: www.shrm.org/Research/MonthlyEmploymentIndices/lmo/Documents/JOS%20Q4%202012.pdf.

Society of Human Resource Management (2012b). *2012 Employee Job Satisfaction and Engagement: How Employees are Dealing with Uncertainty*. SHRM, Alexandria, Virginia.

Society of Human Resource Management (2014). *Tracking Trends in Employee Turnover*. Retrieved from: www.shrm.org/Research/benchmarks/Documents/Trends%20in%20Turnover_FINAL.pdf.

Sonnentag, S., Mojza, E.J., Demerouti, E. and Bakker, A.B. (2012). Reciprocal relations between recovery and work engagement: The moderating role of job stressors. *Journal of Applied Psychology*, 97(4), 842.

Talentkeepers Global Talent and Retention Report 2013. Retrieved from: www.talentkeepers.com/download/2013-TalentKeepers-Employee-Engagement-Retention-Trends-Report-Final.pdf.

Thayer, J.F., Hansen, A.L., Saus-Rose, E., and Johnsen, B.H. (2009). Heart rate variability, prefrontal neural function, and cognitive performance: the neurovisceral integration perspective on self-regulation, adaptation, and health. *Annals of Behavioral Medicine*, 37, 141–53.

Tims, M. and Bakker, A.B. (2010). Job crafting: Towards a new model of individual job redesign. *South African Journal of Industrial Psychology*, 36(2), 1–9.

Tims, M., Bakker, A.B. and Derks, D. (2012). The development and validation of the job crafting scale. *Journal of Vocational Behavior*, 80, 173–86.

Tims, M., Bakker, A.B., and Derks, D. (2013). The impact of job crafting on job demands, job resources, and wellbeing. *Journal of Occupational Health Psychology*, 18, 230–40.

US Department of Labor, Bureau of Statistics (2014a). *Summary of Employment Situation Report*. Retrieved from: www.bls.gov/news.release/empsit.nr0.htm.

US Department of Labor, Bureau of Statistics (2014b).*Turnover and Job Openings Statistics Report February 2014*. Retrieved from: www.bls.gov/news.release/pdf/jolts.pdf.

Van Rooy, D.L., Whitman, D.S., Hart, D. and Caleo, S. (2011). Measuring employee engagement during a financial downturn: business imperative or nuisance? *Journal of Business and Psychology*, 26(2), 147–52.

Vijayakumar, V.T.R. and Parvin, S.A. (2010). Employer branding for sustainable growth of organisations. *International Journal of Enterprise and Innovation Management Studies (IJEIMS)*, 1(3), 10–14.

Warr, P. (2001). Age and work behavior: Physical attributes, cognitive abilities, knowledge, personality traits, and motives. *International Review of Industrial and Organizational Psychology*, 16, 1–36.

Westerman, J.W. and Vanka, S. (2005). A cross-cultural empirical analysis of person-organization fit measures as predictors of student performance in business education: Comparing students in the United States and India. *Academy of Management Learning & Education*, 4(4), 409–20.

Wrzesniewski, A. (2003). Finding positive meaning in work. In K.S. Cameron, J.E. Dutton and R.E. Quinn (eds), *Positive Organizational Scholarship: Foundations of a New Discipline*. Berrett-Koehler, San Francisco, pp. 296–308.

Wrzesniewski, A., LoBuglio, N., Dutton, J.E. and Berg, J.M. (2013). Job crafting and cultivating positive meaning and identity in work. *Advances in Positive Organizational Psychology*, 1, 281–302.

Xanthopoulou, D., Bakker, A.B., Demerouti, E. and Schaufeli, W.B. (2009). Work engagement and financial returns: A diary study on the role of job and personal resources. *Journal of Occupational and Organizational Psychology*, 82(1), 183–200.